LIBERALIZATION AND THE TURKISH ECONOMY

Recent Titles in
Contributions in Economics and Economic History
Series Editor: Robert Sobel

Bridging the Gap Between Rich and Poor: American Economic Development Policy Toward the Arab East, 1942-1949
Nathan Godfried

Rethinking the Nineteenth Century: Contradictions and Movements
Francisco O. Ramirez, editor

Textiles in Transition: Technology, Wages, and Industry Relocation in the U.S. Textile Industry, 1880-1930
Nancy Frances Kane

Threats of Quotas in International Trade: Their Effect on the Exporting Country
Gerard Lawrence Stockhausen

A Slippery Slope: The Long Road to the Breakup of AT&T
Fred W. Henck and Bernard Strassburg

The Suppression of the Automobile: Skulduggery at the Crossroads
David Beasley

New Perspectives on Social Class and Socioeconomic Development in the Periphery
Nelson W. Keith and Novella Zett Keith, editors

World Population Trends and Their Impact on Economic Development
Dominick Salvatore, editor

Racism, Sexism, and the World-System
Joan Smith, Jane Collins, Terence K. Hopkins, and Akbar Muhammad, editors

Electricity in Economic Development: The Experience of Northeast Asia
Yoon Hyung Kim and Kirk R. Smith, editors

LIBERALIZATION AND THE TURKISH ECONOMY

Edited by Tevfik F. Nas and
Mehmet Odekon

Contributions in Economics and
Economic History, Number 86

GREENWOOD PRESS
NEW YORK • WESTPORT, CONNECTICUT • LONDON

Library of Congress Cataloging-in-Publication Data

Liberalization and the Turkish economy / edited by Tevfik F. Nas and Mehmet Odekon.
p. cm. – (Contributions in economics and economic history, ISSN 0084-9235 ; no. 86)
Bibliography: p.
Includes index.
ISBN 0-313-26031-1 (lib. bdg. : alk. paper)
1. Turkey – Economic policy. 2. Economic stabilization – Turkey. I. Nas, Tevfik F. II. Odekon, Mehmet. III. Series.
HC492.L53 1988
338.9561—dc19 88-9755

British Library Cataloguing in Publication Data is available.

Library of Congress Catalog Card Number: 88-9755
ISBN: 0-313-26031-1
ISSN: 0084-9235

First published in 1988

Greenwood Press, Inc.
88 Post Road West, Westport, Connecticut 06881

Printed in the United States of America

The paper used in this book complies with the Permanent Paper Standard issued by the National Information Standards Organization (Z39.48-1984).

10 9 8 7 6 5 4 3 2 1

Contents

Illustrations

FIGURES

TABLES

Acknowledgments

We thank Patrick Conway (University of North Carolina at Chapel Hill), Paula L. Duey (Michigan State University), and Asım Erdilek (Case Western Reserve University) for their help and encouragement in completing this project. We also wish to acknowledge our anonymous reviewer and the staff of the Greenwood Press, especially Cynthia Harris and our production editor Terri Metz. Finally, we thank Judy Bedore who did an excellent job of typing the manuscript and Ginny Egan Lagather (University of Michigan-Flint) for her expert editorial assistance.

The project was partially supported by a Skidmore College Faculty Research Grant and the Economics Department of the University of Michigan-Flint.

Introduction

January 24, 1980, marks an important date in Turkish economic history. Burdened by staggering inflation and an increasingly worsening balance of payments, the government introduced an orthodox stabilization-with-liberalization program under the auspices of the International Monetary Fund. The program included drastic measures to stabilize the economy, encourage export promotion, and gradually remove both trade barriers and foreign exchange restrictions. These radical measures and other structural reforms involving the fiscal system and the financial markets ended fifty years of protectionism and marked the beginning of a period with far-reaching structural changes that could lead to a Western-style free-market economy.

During the first few years, the apparent success of the program was a welcome break from unfavorable reviews of other austerity programs, particularly those implemented in Latin America and other heavily indebted nations. The foreign debt situation improved significantly, and a superior export performance became a leading indicator of progress, as well as a hopeful sign of what more could be accomplished by furthering liberalization efforts in Turkey. As the first seven years come to an end, however, the initial wave of optimism on the potential success of the program, has faded at least for some. Trade and budget deficits remain, and the problems of high inflation and unemployment continue to involve critical "macrochoices."

FREE-MARKET EXPERIMENTS IN TURKEY

The January 24, 1980, program was not the first time that the Turkish economy had experimented with the free-market mechanism. The first attempt, which dates back to the early 1920s, was not as extensive as the recent one and lacked sincere political commitment.[1] A balance of payments crisis in 1926 and a sharp drop in the inflow of short-term capital in 1927 aggravated the foreign exchange shortage, which peaked in 1929 with the Great Depression and ended the era of the free-market economy. A protectionist and statist policy in line with "nationalism," the political ideology of the time, followed (Kazgan 1985).

With the ascent of the Democratic Party to power two decades later, in 1950, the second short-lived free-market experiment began.[2] Taking advantage of the Marshall Plan and easy credit markets, the authorities launched a substantially liberalized trade and payments regime. In the domestic economy, state economic enterprises were put up for sale and price and profit controls were relaxed. However, within two years the pressure of rising inflation on the balance of payments started to be felt. By 1952, overvalued Turkish lira and an increasing trade deficit once again prompted the authorities to resort to protective measures and to shy away from liberalization. During the following two decades, import substitution in various degrees remained the official economic policy.

On August 10, 1970, a substantial devaluation of the Turkish lira started a new phase in the economy.[3] Over the next two years, quantitative and price controls were reduced, and reliance on the market system and incentives for attracting foreign investment were increased. Initially the exchange rate was adjusted to control inflation as well as to attract workers' remittances, the massive inflow of which, with favorable conditions in the credit markets, enabled the economy to share the worldwide boom of 1971-73. Before long this demand-led growth contributed to renewed inflation and also put pressure on the balance of payments, consequently aggravating the debt burden. Up until the second half of the 1970s, however, balance of payments problems remained tolerable because of the workers' remittances. Eventually those remittances diminished rapidly due to the overvaluation of the Turkish lira by

35 to 40 percent and the recession in Europe. In the meantime, the Cypriot conflict aggravated the foreign exchange crisis. In addition to restrictive measures to alleviate the crisis, "convertible currency deposits" (CCDs), a scheme developed in 1967, were also revived.[4]

By 1978, the CCDs had led the economy into a severe crisis, resulting in the June 1979 stabilization program. Adverse developments in the world economy, such as a rise in oil prices and an increase in world interest rates, not only limited any favorable effect the program may have had, but also aggravated domestic and external economic problems.

The pre-1980 liberalization episodes shared some common features (Kazgan 1985):

1. Devaluations, with which these experiments started, led to contractionary effects on the economy, not stimulating exports but restricting imports.
2. All these episodes ended in severe balance of payments and debt crises.
3. In general, domestic savings were not stimulated and foreign investment was always far below the expectations of authorities.
4. Domestic inflation was consistently out of control.
5. All three experiments lacked a direct outward-looking orientation, specifically in terms of stimulating exports. This was partly due to the fact that Turkish exports have traditionally been primary products (with the exception of textiles).

It was especially in this fifth point that the 1980 program differed from the others. Various measures provided direct and indirect incentives for exports:[5]

1. Abolishment of quantitative controls on exports, such as licensing
2. Abolishment of price controls
3. Reimbursements to exporters of indirect taxes incurred, through export tax rebates
4. Various credit facilities with relatively lower interest rates for manufacturers of exportables
5. Permission to retain foreign exchange earnings to use for importing the inputs used in export production
6. Centralization of the administration of export policies

7. Minimization of bureaucratic involvement in the export sector
8. Adjustment of the exchange rate on a daily basis to stimulate exports

These were certainly radical measures for the Turkish economy. Other provisions of the program included: freeing up imports by lowering or eliminating restrictions; relaxing the laws concerning capital imports and exports to render the climate attractive for foreign investment; and imposing monetary and fiscal discipline to control inflation. A major overhaul in the tax system introduced a value-added tax and lowered personal and corporate income taxes (which in 1985 were increased again). An attempt to form a domestic capital market was interrupted by the collapse of the moneylenders' market and was revived again in 1985. With regard to the labor market, restrictions imposed immediately after the 1980 military takeover have been gradually relaxed but not completely removed.[6]

THE PURPOSE AND THE PLAN OF THE BOOK

This book examines various aspects of Turkey's 1980-87 stabilization and liberalization experience. It includes original essays and updated analyses, each focusing on one aspect of the period in an attempt to generate useful propositions with policy implications. The primary purpose of the book is to outline the problems of liberalization in a highly protective, inward-looking policy environment and explore several prospects that could ease Turkey's transition to an outward-looking free-market economy. Equally important, the book intends to stress the interrelationship between stabilization and liberalization measures and emphasize the importance of organizational, political, and legal parameters for successful implementation of liberalization strategy.

In Chapter 1, F. Şenses provides a detailed review of the January 24, 1980, program. A thorough discussion of the trade and exchange rate regimes is followed by an assessment of the program in terms of its impact on the imbalances in the economy. Chapter 2 examines the Turkish liberalization movement from a comparative perspective. A brief theoretical review of liberalization is followed by a comparative study of the major liberalization policies implemented in Turkey and three Latin American countries.

Chapters 3 and 4 by P. Conway and E. Kumcu, respectively, analyze the effects of liberalization policies on output and inflation from contrasting views. Conway finds the frequent devaluations (considered in isolation) to be inflationary and output reducing while improving the trade deficit. In contrast, Kumcu finds a depreciating domestic currency and a rising real interest rate effective in stimulating output and reducing inflation. In their conclusions, Conway suggests imported-input liberalization, and Kumcu supports the view that the Turkish government can achieve favorable output and balance of payment effects by a well-balanced real interest rate *cum* exchange rate policy and at the same time control inflation with monetary policy.

In Chapter 5, M. Fry studies the money supply process and its relation to inflation and growth over the period 1951-85. A major conclusion of the study is that the real deposit rate of interest could be used effectively as a policy tool to reduce inflation and stimulate growth; the increase in the real deposit rate reduces inflation and positively affects economic growth.

In Chapter 6, L. Rittenberg discusses the impact of liberalization on savings and shows that the 1980-82 increase in autonomous savings was followed by a decrease, in spite of the positive real interest rate. This finding supports Fry's warning that further increases in the real deposit rate could result in higher inflation while simultaneously stimulating growth. Rittenberg also suggests that a positive interest rate must be accompanied by the creation of financial markets to stimulate savings. The issue of restructuring the financial markets, the privatization of State Economic Enterprises, and the opportunity it provides to organize an efficient capital market are discussed in Chapter 7 by I. Inselbag and B. Gültekin.

The failure to mobilize domestic savings raises the need for foreign capital. Chapters 8 and 9 are devoted to this issue, analyzing the problems and prospects for Turkey in raising funds in international financial markets. In Chapter 8, A. Erdilek focuses on the effects of liberalization on foreign direct investment in Turkey. Despite some favorable increases in the inflow of private capital, this inflow has been below the expectations of the authorities. A possible cause of such performance, Erdilek argues, is the government's own unstable policymaking and the uneven pace of the economy's development. In Chapter 9, D. Rodrik shares similar concerns. Rodrik analyzes the causes of the 1977 debt crisis, Turkey's relation to foreign capital markets, and its export performance in the post-1977 era. He concludes that unless an increase in private investment in the tradable goods sector is realized and overall confidence in the state of the economy is maintained, the flow of capital is likely to diminish and the export boom will come to an end.

Finally, Chapter 10 provides a combined summary of the preceding chapters, explores two likely departures from the status quo, and concludes with useful suggestions concerning the future of Turkey's liberalization movement.

NOTES

1. For a detailed review of the 1923-26 period, see Kazgan (1985).

2. For a full account of the 1950-70 period, see Kazgan (1985) and Krueger (1974, 1978).

3. It is interesting to note that the 1970 devaluation had little effect on exports but did increase the inflow of capital; see Kazgan (1985).

4. CCDs are deposits held in convertible currencies in Turkish commercial banks. The exchange rate risk is eliminated by public guarantee. Let it suffice to indicate here that CCDs were tied to flexible interest rates and were mainly used to finance the imports of consumer durables.

5. See OECD, Economic Survey (various issues in and after 1980) and Milanovic (1986).

6. For the details of the January 24, 1980, program, see Ulagay (1983), Çölaşan (1983), Sönmez (1982), and Şenses (1983).

REFERENCES

Çölaşan, E. 1983. *24 Ocak, Bir Donemin Perde Arkasi.* Istanbul: Milliyet Yayinlari.

Kazgan, G. 1985. *Ekonomide Disa Acik Buyume.* Istanbul: Altin Kitaplar.

Krueger, A. O. 1974. *Foreign Trade Regimes and Economic Development: Turkey.* New York: National Bureau of Economic Research.

______. 1978. *Liberalization Attempts and Consequences.* New York: National Bureau of Economic Research.

Milanovic, B. 1986. Export incentives and Turkish manufactured exports, 1980-84. World Bank Staff Paper 768. Washington, D.C.: The World Bank.

Şenses, F. 1983. An assessment of Turkey's liberalization attempts since 1980 against the background of her stabilization program. *METU Studies in Development* 10(3):271-322.

Sönmez, M. 1982. *Turkiye Ekonomisinde Bunalim* 2d. ed. Istanbul: Belge Yayinlari.

Ulagay, O. 1983. *24 Ocak Deneyimi Uzerine*. Istanbul: Hil Yayin.

1

An Overview of Recent Turkish Experience with Economic Stabilization and Liberalization

FIKRET ŞENSES

After the mid-sixties, Turkey's traditional industrialization strategy, based on import substitution through protectionist policies, was increasingly constrained by a foreign exchange bottleneck. The problem, which arose basically from the low level of exports in the face of heavy dependence on imports of production and investment goods by the manufacturing sector, was aggravated by successive oil shocks in the 1970s, and led toward the end of that decade to rampant inflation and a full-scale payments crisis. The inability of two stabilization programs to deal with the crisis culminated in the introduction in January 1980 of an orthodox stabilization program under the auspices of the International Monetary Fund (IMF), a program which received immediate recognition and support from international organizations like the World Bank and the Organization for Economic Cooperation and Development (OECD).[1] The program, which represented by far the most significant break from earlier policies, received a major boost from the establishment of a military government in September 1980. This enabled the program's continued enforcement during the full course of military rule, which ended following the November 1983 general elections. The elections resulted in a sweeping victory by a new political party founded and led by members of the economic team closely associated with the program. The most significant element in the implementation of the program after this date was the radical shift in policies vis-à-vis foreign trade and payments toward liberalization and an increased export orientation in the economy.

The main objective of this chapter is to give an overview of the characteristics and main impact of economic policies making up the Stabilization Program in force since January 1980, with particular emphasis on liberalization attempts. In an effort to evaluate the package within the context of long-term goals and experience, we look beyond the short-term implications of the program and provide some insights into the medium- and long-term prospects of the economy. The first section provides a brief overview of economic policies followed during 1980-86 with an assessment of their impact. This is followed by an evaluation of the nature and extent of liberalization attempts since 1980. Prospects and conclusions are presented in the last section.

THE STABILIZATION PROGRAM, 1980-86

Liberalization attempts during 1980-86 were introduced as a part of and with direct reference to the Stabilization Program. While a comprehensive evaluation of the program is beyond the scope of this study, it is essential to provide a brief account of that program to serve as background to our more detailed assessment of liberalization attempts in the next section.

Two essential characteristics of the program merit attention at the outset. First, despite frequent official pronouncements to the contrary, the program showed a great deal of resemblance to orthodox stabilization packages introduced in a number of other countries, often by authoritarian governments and under IMF auspices.[2] Second, although previous stabilization efforts in Turkey bore a resemblance to the 1980 program vis-à-vis the circumstances which led to their introduction, the set of policies implemented, and the role of international agencies as donors of aid, the significance of the 1980 program and the controversy surrounding it outweighed those of earlier efforts.[3] This can be attributed largely to the fact that Turkish governments viewed the earlier programs as merely short-term expedients to provide fresh facilities and get them out of the immediate impasse. Once the impasse was over, the government would backtrack from the programs and violate their stipulations. In contrast, given growing disenchantment with traditional strategy in Turkey, the 1980 program was more readily welcomed and was implemented over a longer period of time with much greater firmness and determination.[4]

Although initially introduced as a short-term stabilization package to tackle primarily the twin problems of inflation and balance of payments difficulties, the program was characterized by a multiplicity of objectives with short- and long-term connotations. These objectives may be classified under five main headings, with the first three generally referring to the short term: (1) eliminating disequilibria in major markets and breaking the inflationary spiral; (2) coping with immediate pressures on the balance of payments; (3) reducing inflation and attaining price stability; (4) privatizing economic life; and (5) liberalizing foreign trade and payments as a part of efforts to shift to an export-oriented industrialization strategy and attain a sustainable balance of payments position. Although there was some variation in the degree of importance attached to these objectives over time, the variety of policies implemented under the program constituted a remarkably uniform set. Uniformity occurred because IMF performance criteria were the overriding influence in the selection of economic policies in a wide range of spheres, particularly in the field of monetary, fiscal, trade, and industrialization policies.

The overall record of the Stabilization Program, after more than seven years of uninterrupted implementation, was a mixed one with remarkable achievements in several spheres and poor results in others. The rate of growth of Gross National Product (GNP) averaged 5.1 percent during 1981-86 which, although not high in relation to rates achieved during the previous two decades, was a remarkable improvement over the virtual stagnation experienced during 1978-80.[5] More significant was an extraordinary growth in exports, which increased (in billion dollars) from 2.9 in 1980 to 5.7 in 1982 and 7.5 in 1986. This was accompanied by a sharp shift in export composition toward manufactures and by market expansion to include Middle Eastern and North African countries. (The share of manufactures in total exports during 1982-86 averaged 69.8 percent as opposed to 32.6 percent during 1978-80. Similarly, the share of Middle Eastern and North African countries rose from an average of 20.2 percent during 1979-80 to 41.8 percent during

1982-86.) Apart from the government's commitment to an all-out export drive and the favorable treatment accorded exporters, the success of this drive, at a time of an unfavorable external environment, owed much to slack domestic demand, along with exchange rate flexibility and other export promotion schemes. This shift in emphasis toward an export orientation was also reflected in the share of exports in GNP, which increased from 3.8 percent during 1977-79 to 13.6 percent during 1983-86. With imports growing, albeit at a slow pace, and workers' remittances unstable and declining in recent years, the growth of exports was largely instrumental in keeping the current account deficit at a modest level. As a share of exports, the current account deficit fell from 106.4 percent in 1980 to 14.5 percent in 1982, 19.7 percent in 1984, 12.7 percent in 1985, and 20.5 percent in 1986. After a sharp reduction in 1981 and 1982, the rate of inflation, on the other hand, could not be reduced below 25 percent and averaged 37.3 percent during 1983-86 as a whole. The lack of success on this front has not, however, deterred Turkey's donors from hailing its economic record as a major success, which in turn contributed to considerable improvement in its creditworthiness in the international financial community during this period. As a result, external credits from a variety of sources, most notably from the OECD, IMF, World Bank, certain OPEC countries, and the international banking community, provided much of the balance of payments support.

Apart from the lack of success on the inflationary front, performance under the program was far less than satisfactory in a number of areas. Critics increasingly draw attention to the program's poor record with respect to unemployment and income distribution. Estimates of the rate of unemployment based on surplus labor in both the agricultural and nonagricultural sectors indicated an upward tendency, with the rate rising from 14.0 percent in 1979 to an average of 16.8 percent during 1982-86. This was reinforced by Turkish Employment Service data on open unemployment which indicated more than a threefold increase during 1981-86. Although the rise in unemployment in absolute terms was partly due to structural factors like the still rapid increase in population growth (2.4 percent per annum, on average, during 1965-85), and, therefore, not directly attributable to the program, it can safely be argued that the slowdown in the pace of employment creation, especially in the public sector, also aggravated already severe pressures in the labor market. This reflected the government's reluctance to improve employment because of its increased concern with the efficiency of State Economic Enterprises (SEEs), generally characterized by overstaffing. While the lack of data has precluded analysis of expenditure categories with strong welfare connotations like housing, education, and health, the data on the sectoral distribution of total fixed capital formation during 1984-86 indicate a slight rise in housing and no significant change in health and education. Despite the absence of more systematic data covering the whole period, there is evidence of a worsening of income distribution during this period: a rising rate of unemployment together with a sharp fall in real wages and salaries (Table 1.1); a large reduction in the share of wages and salaries in manufacturing value added; and the removal of subsidies on a large number of essential goods and services produced by the SEEs. The inability so far to generate a sustained increase in saving and investment rates and attain structural change in the sectoral composition of aggregate output and investment constitute another sphere in which the program fell short of expectations. The virtual constancy of the share in aggregate production of industry in general and manufacturing in particular was taken, for example, as evidence to halt the industrialization process. Similarly, the marked shift under the program in investment composition from manufacturing toward such sectors as agriculture, transport, and energy were identified as developments which would, if prolonged, have an adverse medium- and long-term development impact.

AN ASSESSMENT OF LIBERALIZATION ATTEMPTS SINCE 1980

Although official statements since the early days of the Stabilization Program reflect a growing preoccupation with trade liberalization and the need to give the economy an outward orientation, one is struck by the absence of any well-publicized plan or prior warning about the government's specific intentions vis-à-vis liberalization. While a decrease in the importance attached to comprehensive central planning after 1980 may partly account for this, one learns from

TABLE 1.1 Selected Economic Indicators, 1978-86

Year	GNP[a]	Investment Rate[b]	Real Wages[c]	Unemployment Rate[d]	Wholesale Prices[e]
1978	209.2	21.7	50.94	-	52.6
1979	208.3	21.8	40.93	14.0	63.9
1980	206.1	19.5	29.49	15.4	107.2
1981	214.6	18.5	32.78	16.8	36.7
1982	224.5	18.9	30.93	18.2	25.3
1983	231.9	18.5	31.70	16.1	30.6
1984	245.6	18.4	n.a.	16.1	52.0
1985	258.1	19.6	n.a.	16.7	40.0
1986	278.1*	22.4*	n.a.	16.8	26.7

Sources: Central Bank, *Annual Report*, various issues, unless otherwise stated.

*Refers to provisional estimates.

[a]Billion TL in purchasers' prices at constant prices of 1968; State Institute of Statistics (1983:481) for 1978-81.

[b]Percentage ratio of gross fixed investment to GNP in purchasers' prices (both at current prices).

[c]Real net wages in liras per day obtained by deflating nominal wages by the Istanbul cost of living index.

[d]Percentage ratio of total surplus labor to total civilian labor supply, Ministry of Finance, *Annual Economic Report*, various issues.

[e]Percentage change over the previous year, based on 1963 = 100.

an IMF document (IMF 1982b:14) that a number of industry studies were ". . . under way which will provide a basis for the selective easing of import restrictions" and that the general import regime was to be "liberalized significantly further from January 1983." The reluctance to pre-announce import liberalization measures notwithstanding, even a cursory examination of stabilization policies since 1980 reveals at least two areas with a strong bearing on liberalization attempts, indicating that such attempts were characterized by a degree of gradualism that could be traced to the early days of the program.

First, preoccupation with trade liberalization, especially in the initial years of the program, and with short-term objectives like coping with galloping inflation and severe balance of payments difficulties, entailed (1) resorting to external borrowing and (2) relying on demand restraint through tight monetary and fiscal policies. It can be argued that both of these factors have contributed positively to the process of import liberalization. The first contributed by sharply reducing waiting periods for import licenses and facilitating an increased flow of imports, and the second did so largely through its role in increasing the export supply while curbing the demand for imports, especially by redirecting resources from relatively more import-dependent activities at a time of low rates of growth of domestic economic activity.

Second, there was a marked tendency toward liberalization and giving the economy an increased export orientation through the introduction of new measures in a number of key areas of the trade and payments regime. During the first year of the Stabilization Program, for example, with primary emphasis on export promotion, efforts on the import front consisted of a sharp reduction in stamp duty, guaranteed deposits on imports, and considerable simplification of import procedures (IMF 1981:426). More significant, this was followed by the abolition in January 1981 of the list of goods subject to global quotas, which had represented 12 percent of total imports in 1980 (IMF 1982a:444). Similarly, the 1983 import program stipulated that all import transactions were to be carried out on the basis of convertible foreign currencies. This process toward a more liberal import regime culminated in the 1984 import regime, which signaled a transition from a positive to a negative list and a major downward revision of production tax rates and tariffs extending into 59 BTN chapters (Şenses 1983:289-305). Parallel to these developments, macroeconomic policies were simultaneously aimed at lowering import demand and raising export supply to facilitate an increase in import capacity. To serve the latter objective, the government relied on a variety of export-promotion measures like tax rebates, import replenishment and foreign exchange retention schemes, and provision of export credits at preferential rates for production, and investment in export activities. These were accompanied by a gradual liberalization of the export regime, the simplification of procedures guiding exportation, and the granting of export incentives. A major factor that became increasingly evident on the export front during this period was that exporters were favorably treated in their dealings with public agencies. Official pronouncements throughout the period reflected a wholehearted commitment to export orientation.

Changes with respect to export and import regimes were accompanied by a degree of relaxation in exchange control regulations. Following growing emphasis on exchange rate flexibility during 1980-83, measures designed to be a major step in the direction of making the lira a fully convertible currency in the not too distant future were introduced in December 1983. Under the new regulations commercial banks were allowed to determine their buying and selling rates within a margin of 6 percent above or below the rate determined by the Central Bank.[6] As a result of the failure to make sufficient progress on the inflation front, a growing emphasis on exchange rate flexibility enabled the government to proceed uninterrupted with its trade liberalization and export orientation objectives. Although the depreciation of the lira during 1980-83 was accompanied by tax and credit incentives for exports, there was a parallel move toward increased reliance on the exchange rate in this respect. The emphasis on exchange rate flexibility and unification was instrumental in wiping out black markets in foreign exchange and reducing import premiums and represented a major element in liberalization attempts, especially through its favorable impact on import capacity via export growth. In the pursuit of the latter objective, there were two additional developments which may be regarded as a further reflection of the government's commitment to the export drive. First, as a part of its emphasis on the need to export in larger volumes, the government encouraged consolidation of exporting firms, further simplified export procedures, and called for the cooperation of the government bureaucracy for the success of the export drive.[7] Second, official visits to various countries became much more closely linked with the export drive, and in many cases officials were accompanied by a strong team of exporting industrialists.

After the major boost given by the 1984 import regime, liberalization attempts continued on a broad front during 1984-86. The trend toward a more liberal import regime during this period was strengthened by a reduction in import guarantee deposit rates, the elimination of a production tax on imports, and the abolition of a 5 percent surcharge on imports from European Economic Community (EEC) countries. Another significant development in the import sphere was a new tariff revision in December 1985 (extending into 88 BTN chapters and covering mostly items not covered in the 1983 revision), reflecting an overall reduction in customs duties (Resmi Gazete, 26 December 1985). In an effort to remove the differential incentives granted to competing activities by the import regime, exemptions from customs duties, taxes, and fees on imports by public sector entities were abolished in 1986. Furthermore, increased liberalization of international capital transactions and the easing of foreign exchange regulations in 1984 have, in subsequent years, led to a rapid expansion of foreign currency denominated assets and liabilities by Turkish commercial banks (OECD 1986:34-6).

On the export front, there was a marked tendency for further exchange rate unification with various export incentives gradually removed. Thus rebate rates ranging from 2.75 percent to 11.0 percent of export value were lowered at the end of 1984, and preferential export credits were eliminated the following year (IMF 1985:500). This was accompanied, however, by an extension of the period that exporters could keep their foreign currency holdings (from ten days to three months) and, much more significant, by depreciation of the real exchange rate.[8]

As it is clear from our examination so far, liberalization attempts since 1980 have represented a gradual and cautious process. These attempts, which initially relied mostly on the transfer of various items from the restricted to the more liberalized lists, have, especially after the abolition of quotas in early 1981, entailed a growing emphasis on relying on price measures, most notably the exchange rate, rather than quantitative restrictions in the regulation of the balance of payments. Furthermore, liberalization attempts have proceeded along a broad front, encompassing all major import categories. Decisive and highly significant measures like the transition to a negative list, involving a considerable extension in the list of commodities that can be imported, have been implemented, as have major tariff revisions. Revisions have included a significant reduction in tariff rates and in the variance of tariffs within individual import categories. Although a portion of imports remained subject to licensing and approval by public agencies, this should not lead one to underestimate the considerable progress made toward liberalization, especially in view of the long periods of highly restrictive import policies before 1980.

Objectives and Chances of Success of Liberalization Attempts

An examination of official declarations on the subject and measures actually introduced leads one to conclude that liberalization attempts were prompted by a multiplicity of objectives which may be classified under two broad and interrelated headings: (1) attainment of a sustainable balance of payments position through export orientation and (2) reduction of domestic inflation, basically through a more efficient allocation of resources. Replacement of quantitative restrictions with price measures and the simplification of the trade and payments regime would, it was hoped, reduce the high rates of protection prevalent in manufacturing and make producers more conscious of the cost and quality of their products, thereby increasing their competitiveness in world markets.[9] Along with a drop in the prices of inputs used in export production following liberalization, this was expected to reduce the bias against exports and give the economy an increased export orientation. Competition provided by an increased flow of imports, on the other hand, was expected to reduce monopolistic and oligopolistic tendencies--especially in activities where the domestic market was too small for efficient production--thereby eliminating import premiums and excessive profits and exerting downward pressure on prices.[10] This was particularly the case in some "luxury" consumption goods which, as a result of their exclusion from permissible import lists over long periods of time, were generally characterized by high import premiums and smuggling. By allowing their importation, the government seemed to have the dual purpose of redirecting transactions into official channels and taxing luxury consumption. Furthermore, by linking popular demands like increased emphasis on housing projects with the (excise) taxes collected from the importation of these commodities and from foreign travel by Turkish nationals, the government probably hoped to broaden support for its liberalization policy.

Despite the short period of time that has elapsed since liberalization attempts have gained real momentum, a number of observations can be made about their initial and likely future impact in the light of the objectives stated above. One can argue that the considerable progress made in import liberalization and the provision of substantial tax and credit incentives to exporters were instrumental in reducing the anti-export bias of the trade regime in most activities while probably reversing it in some others, particularly in traditional branches like food and textiles, which received a major portion of export incentives. In contrast, not much headway in this context was made on the inflation front. While tariff reductions, particularly for intermediate goods, may exert downward pressure on prices, the same cannot be said for consumption goods, especially for luxury items. Given the highly skewed distribution of income, demand for these items is probably heavily concentrated in higher-income groups. Thus, it seems that imports of much higher quality and at much higher prices are not directly competing with domestic substitutes. It is unlikely, therefore, that these items, which are well beyond the reach of even middle income groups, will be imported in sufficiently large quantities to significantly alter the behavior of domestic firms in the short term. Given the high degree of responsiveness of firms to government threats (or action) that imports will be resorted to in order to prevent "undue price hikes," it seems that progress in the use of import liberalization as an instrument of anti-inflationary policy will, in the future, depend on the actual scale of imports as well as on the extension and sustainability of liberalization attempts.

Prospects for the Sustainability of Liberalization Attempts

In view of the failure of many liberalization attempts in Turkey and elsewhere,[11] it is worth considering the chances of success and sustainability of these attempts from both a short- and medium-term perspective. Short-term prospects are surrounded by a number of issues pertaining to the timing of and likely response to these attempts.

Timing and Initial Response: Although the postponement of major attempts at liberalization until after some progress was made with such pressing short-term problems as galloping inflation and severe pressures on the balance of payments was understandable, a number of doubts can still be expressed about the timing of major attempts at liberalization which in earnest began with the 1984 import regime.

1. Considerable progress made during 1980-83 on the balance of payments front notwithstanding, certain developments in trade, especially after the first quarter of 1983, did not fare well. Total export receipts stagnated after the peak reached in the previous year, and there was further deterioration in external terms of trade in 1983 (see Table 1.2). Furthermore, despite continued growth in international reserves during 1983, even the peak reached in November was equivalent to less than three months of 1983 imports, a situation compounded by increasing debt service obligations in the next few years.[12]
2. The failure to reduce inflation below 30 percent at the end of four years of stabilization efforts was aggravated by a significant acceleration in that rate after the first quarter of 1983. The fact that 1983 was a bad year for agriculture was another example of unfortunate timing and may have raised inflationary expectations. A related point was the possibility that exportable surplus could be reaching its limits in certain lines of activity, thus bringing into the foreground the possibility of a trade-off between further export growth and reduction in the domestic rate of inflation.
3. Liberalization attempts coincided with a period of rising unemployment and low rates of growth in

TABLE 1.2 Selected Balance of Payments Transactions, 1978-86

Year	Imports[a]	Total Exports[a]	Workers Remittances[a]	Terms of Trade[b]	Reserves[c]
1978	4599	2288	983	73.8	711
1979	5069	2261	1694	73.7	706
1980	7909	2910	2071	56.9	1209
1981	8933	4703	2490	52.1	1658
1982	8843	5746	2140	49.7	2027
1983	9235	5728	1513	49.0	2253
1984	10757	7133	1807	55.3	3899
1985	11344	7958	1714	n.a.	3655
1986	11105	7457	1634*	n.a.	4424

Sources: Central Bank, *Annual Report*, various issues, unless otherwise stated.

*Refers to provisional estimates.

[a]Million dollars.

[b]Percentage ratio of export prices to import prices based on dollar prices (1973 = 100). The index was not published for the last two years of the series.

[c]Billion dollars, reflects the sum of gold and gross foreign exchange reserves.

domestic demand and output, especially in agriculture. This was accompanied by unfavorable trends in the international economy, characterized by slow growth in production and trade and widespread recourse to protectionist measures.

Doubts about the timing of liberalization attempts were outweighed, however, by three main premises by which the government appeared to have been strongly influenced. First, to the extent that policies implemented as a part of the liberalization process and the Stabilization Program were mutually reinforcing, the wisdom of introducing these attempts amid stabilization efforts and, indeed, as an integral and internally consistent part of those efforts is self-evident. While the pursuit of strict monetary and fiscal policies, low rates of growth accompanied by the discouragement of import-dependent production and investment, and depreciation in the real rate of exchange have helped curb the demand for imports, increased export orientation generated through a variety of incentives was, by channeling resources into export activities, expected to increase export receipts and thereby sustain liberalization attempts. This was reinforced by emphasizing product and market diversification in export growth in an attempt to contain the adverse effects of protectionism in major importing countries. The second basic premise on which the government's defense of its timing of liberalization attempts appeared to rest was the support of international organizations like the World Bank and the IMF which, having played an important role in the shaping of Turkish stabilization and liberalization efforts since 1980, were beginning to identify themselves more closely with this experiment. This was accompanied by a considerable improvement in Turkey's creditworthiness in the eyes of international private banks.

The third and perhaps the most significant premise in this context stemmed from domestic political considerations. The fact that the first steps in the direction of liberalization corresponded with the beginning of military rule and gained momentum during the 1984 import regime when the government's political support was at its peak seems to corroborate this view. Partly as a result of this and despite the initial controversy liberalization attempts had generated, they have constituted one sphere of the Stabilization Program characterized by an apparent lack of concerted criticism, especially from the private sector. The relative silence of the private sector, which had been influential in the direction taken by economic policies and outspoken on issues like the shortage and price of bank credit, may be adduced to several factors.

1. Given daily adjustments in the exchange rate and the still high duties, levies, and other charges on imports, it was perhaps thought that the scale of imports in the newly liberalized categories would

not reach sizeable proportions, an expectation to some extent reinforced by the early import response.[13]

2. One can speculate that the private sector's relative silence on the subject was not so much due to the absence of any real grievances as it was to reluctance to confront the government, which was heavily committed to pursuing the privatization objective. A related factor was the apparent variety of private sector views, with exporting industrialists and some commercial interests in export and import activities no doubt pleased with Turkey's greater export orientation, while sections of import-substituting interests also expressed some similar convictions.
3. In the broader support of liberalization attempts by the public at large there were additional elements. Apart from its shrewdness in linking liberalization attempts with projects like housing, the government rallied support by also linking them with popular anti-inflationary, anti-trust, and consumer protection objectives and proposals included in its economic program.

PROSPECTS AND CONCLUSIONS

Liberalization attempts in Turkey, as in many other countries, started during a stabilization crisis and gained momentum after some progress toward stability had been attained. An element of gradualism and surprise has characterized these attempts as it has the Stabilization Program itself.

The factors that will determine the sustainability and ultimate success of liberalization attempts pertain to the medium and long term and have strong socio-political as well as economic connotations in a number of key areas. First, the continued backing of the IMF and the World Bank, along with the OECD and international private banks, is crucial for balance of payments support. An important safeguard for the future success of liberalization attempts, and indeed for the Stabilization Program as a whole, is the expectation that these organizations may provide fresh facilities to sustain the program and even back Turkey should it face renewed pressures in its balance of payments.

Second, and more significant, the government's

assessment of short- and medium-term balance of payments prospects, particularly in relation to exports, will be a crucial determinant of the pace and sustainability of liberalization attempts in the years ahead. Although a detailed examination of Turkey's exports is beyond the scope of this chapter, it is likely that trends in the world economy, particularly in the economies of its likely trade partners, will have a great deal of bearing on export performance. The available evidence of this, however, is uncertain. The poor growth performance of OECD countries in recent years has been accompanied by increased protectionism, particularly severe in (traditional) labor-intensive lines of production. Given the concentration of Turkish exports on these lines, it is a foregone conclusion that protectionist tendencies in industrial countries will continue to adversely impact export growth, which may be aggravated by similar trends in middle and low income countries. Likewise, uncertainties surrounding the Iran-Iraq War, as well as international oil prices after a recent downward trend, do not bode well for Turkey's export prospects given the sizeable number of neighboring oil-exporting countries to which it exports. Despite these unfavorable trends, the government's continued emphasis on export growth may succeed in sustaining recent performance, which was not only unprecedented in Turkey but also high by international standards, particularly if the emphasis on product and market diversification is maintained. On the import front, prospects are closely interwoven with sectoral composition as well as with the rate of future growth. One may argue that the recent revival of interest in the objective of growth may not lead to a big surge in imports despite continued import liberalization. This is due to changes in the sectoral composition of production and new investment which has increasingly emphasized the channeling of resources into relatively less import-dependent activities and into export industries reflecting Turkey's comparative advantage.

There are two factors that have a close bearing on the sustainability of liberalization attempts. First, although slow progress on the inflation front has been regarded as a common characteristic of stabilization policies in general, the failure to control inflation after more than seven years of an orthodox stabilization program based on monetary control and severe restraint on the real incomes of a large section of the population (most notably wage and salary earners) is likely to remain a highly significant and controversial feature of the program. Second, as the external backing of the program has been conditional on a strict adherence to it by the government, the sustainability of liberalization attempts in the medium term is likely to be heavily constrained by domestic political considerations. In view of the fact that liberalization attempts have been an integral part of the Stabilization Program, loss of domestic political support by the government on that count may bring those attempts to a halt and even lead to a return to earlier policies. Such an outcome would naturally entail the loss of potential benefits expected to accrue from the considerable progress made so far toward liberalization and export orientation. It is against such a possibility that policymakers should reassess the record of the Stabilization Program with less self-righteousness and seek alternative approaches with much greater concern about the welfare of the social groups that lost heavily during the more than seven years of uninterrupted stabilization.

NOTES

This paper is a revised and updated version of Şenses (1981,1983). The author wishes to thank T. Nas for his constructive comments on the paper and encouragement.

1. For details on Turkey's relations with the IMF during this period, see Ramazanoglu (1985:91-94) and Berksoy (1982:159-69).

2. For details on stabilization programs in other countries, see Cline and Weintraub (1981).

3. For a thorough evaluation of the Turkish stabilization program of 1958 and the 1970 devaluation package, see Krueger (1974:63-116 and 309-24).

4. In his comparative study of Turkish stabilization programs, Ekzen (1984:180) draws attention to the fact that four stabilization programs lasting a total of seven years were implemented during 1958-80. This shows that the present program has already outlasted previous attempts by a big margin.

5. Statistical information given in this section is based on data given in Ministry of Finance, *Annual Economic Report*, various issues; Central Bank, *Annual Report*, various issues; Central Bank, *Quarterly*

Statistical Summary; and our Tables 1.1 and 1.2.

6. The margin was reduced to 1 percent in March 1986 after some banks had offered very high premiums over the Central Bank rate, leading to speculation against the lira. For details see OECD (1986:37).

7. The following statement from the 1984 Export Regime (Resmi Gazete, 29 December:37) is rather telling in this respect. ". . . staff of public and professional agencies are required to take the necessary measures and provide facilities to increase exports and complete transactions with speed. No staff member can, under the pretext of carrying out his duties, hinder the activities of the exporter."

8. According to OECD (1986:24), the rate of depreciation in real terms averaged around 10 percent (December 1981 = 100) in recent years, with a maximum decline of about 20 percent reached in March 1984 and the second half of 1985.

9. The Government Program published in Resmi Gazete (25 December 1983) stated succinctly that "the government considers it imperative to make the transition from import substitution to export orientation and to an industrialization policy to integrate (domestic industry) to world industry and trade."

10. The link between liberalization and control of inflation objectives was well illustrated by the following statement from the Government Program (Resmi Gazete, 25 December 1983): "There will be a gradual liberalization of imports to enable the consumer to buy cheap and quality products."

11. See Krueger (1978:Ch. 9 and 219-20) for a discussion of successes and failures in liberalization attempts in various countries.

12. According to information given in Central Bank (1984:39-41), the ratio of total payments of principal and interest as a ratio of exports and invisibles (net of interest payments), which indicated a marked increase in 1982, rose again in 1983 and reached its peak for 1979-83.

13. The fact that total imports registered only slow growth during 1983-86 should not conceal the fact that by far the largest increase was in the category of consumption goods, whose share in total imports rose from 2.6 percent in 1983 to 4.4 percent in 1984 and 8.6 percent in 1986 (Central Bank, *Annual Report*, 1986:135). It must be noted, however, that a part of the

"luxury" goods included in the newly liberalized categories were smuggled into the country prior to liberalization.

REFERENCES

Berksoy, T. 1982. Türkiye'de istikrar arayişlari ve IMF. In *IMF Istikrar Politikalari ve Turkiye*, edited by C. Erdost. Ankara: Savaş Yayinlari.

Central Bank of the Republic of Turkey. *Annual Report*. Various issues. Ankara.

______. 1984. *Information Memorandum*. Ankara, June.

Cline, W. R., and S. Weintraub, eds. 1981. *Economic Stabilization in Developing Countries*. Washington, D.C.: The Brookings Institution.

Ekzen, N. 1984. 1980 stabilizasyon paketinin 1958, 1970 ve 1978-1979 paketleri ile karsilastirmali analizi. In *Turkiye'de ve Dunyada Yasanan Ekonomik Bunalim*, edited by I. Tekeli, et al. Ankara: Yurt Yayinlari.

International Monetary Fund. 1981. *Annual Report on Exchange Arrangements and Exchange Restrictions, 1981*. Washington, D. C.: International Monetary Fund.

______. 1982a. *Exchange Arrangements and Exchange Restrictions, Annual Report 1982*. Washington, D. C.: International Monetary Fund.

______. 1982b. Turkey--review of stand-by arrangement and exchange system. EBS/82/130. Washington, D. C.: International Monetary Fund.

______. 1985. *Exchange Arrangements and Exchange Restrictions, Annual Report 1985*. Washington, D. C.: International Monetary Fund.

Krueger, A. 1974. *Foreign Trade Regimes and Economic Development: Turkey*. New York: National Bureau of Economic Research.

______. 1978. *Foreign Trade Regimes and Economic Development: Liberalization Attempts and Consequences.* New York: Columbia University Press.

Ministry of Finance. *Annual Economic Report.* Various issues. Ankara.

Organization for Economic Cooperation and Development. *Turkey--Annual Economic Survey.* Various issues. Paris: OECD.

Ramazanoglu, H. 1985. The politics of industrialization in a closed economy and the IMF intervention of 1979. In *Turkey in the World Capitalist System,* edited by H. Ramazanoglu. Aldershot Eng.: Gower.

Şenses, F. 1981. Short-term stabilization policies in a developing economy: The Turkish experience in 1980 in long-term perspective. *METU Studies in Development* 8(1-2):409-52.

______. 1983. An assessment of Turkey's liberalization attempts since 1980 against the background of her stabilization program. *METU Studies in Development* 10(3):271-322.

State Institute of Statistics. 1983. *Statistical Yearbook of Turkey, 1983.* Ankara.

T. C. Resmi Gazete (Official Gazette of the Turkish Republic). Various issues. Ankara.

2

Liberalization and the Turkish Economy: A Comparative Analysis

MEHMET ODEKON

This chapter examines Turkish liberalization efforts from a comparative perspective. The first section presents a theoretical outline of liberalization. The second section compares and contrasts the major liberalization policies implemented in Turkey with those from selected Latin American economies, and the third section concludes the study.

ECONOMIC LIBERALIZATION

Economic liberalization refers to the opening of an economy to free-market forces. Within the context of contemporary development economics, it is perceived more in terms of the liberalization of the trade and/or capital accounts in the economy with domestic goods and/or assets markets implicitly assumed to follow suit. Thus, a pragmatic working definition of liberalization would be a policy that reduces or eliminates restrictions on foreign trade and/or capital transactions.[1]

The origin of "liberalization" lies in the infamous "trade as an engine of growth" argument. In its simplest form, based on the theory of comparative advantage, the argument emphasizes the prospects of increased economic efficiency, of economies of scale, as well as of rises in real output, consumption, investment, and employment once an economy engages in free trade, specializing in the production of goods in which it has a comparative advantage. This pro-trade argument has been challenged by the structuralists, dependency advocates, and protectionists. Students of development economics in the 1960s were extensively exposed to this literature. In the 1960s, with the exception of Brazil, the implementation of free-trade policies were concentrated in Southeast Asia. In the 1970s, on the other hand, mainly with the collaboration of the IMF, the implementation of liberalization policies as a development strategy spread into the Southern Cone countries in Latin America.

This 1970s version of the "engine of growth" approach, also referred to as "stabilization-with-liberalization," differs from the orthodox free-trade argument in that it emphasizes resource allocation and structural adjustment and, hence, considers short- as well as long-run problems of development. The supply effects expected from liberalization of the external sector of the economy stemmed from the belief that export promotion would lead to an improvement in the balance of payments that, in turn, would favorably affect the imports of capital goods, raw materials, and other inputs, expanding the supply capacity of the economy (Khan and Zahler 1987). Meanwhile, liberalization of capital transactions would lead to higher savings and investment. The liberalization component of the policy package is combined with restrictive fiscal and monetary policies and a "realistic" exchange rate policy to control aggregate demand and inflation in the ailing economy. In short, the idea is to expand supply along a stable demand with no adverse effects on inflation, but with favorable effects on output, employment, and balance of payments.

Arguments against liberalization abound. It is said, for instance, that successful liberalization examples (with the exception of Brazil and mainly concentrated in Southeast Asia) exist from the 1950-70 period when Western industrialized economies were experiencing rapid growth. Hence, export-led growth strategy could work in the presence of strong external demand. It is maintained that the poor performance of the industrialized world since the 1970s restricts the demand for manufactured imports from developing nations and would prevent the repetition of the Southeast Asian success episode (Cline 1982).

An important aspect of liberalization is the realization that it is a policy that requires a long-term perspective which foresees the elimination of barriers on all present and future goods (Calvo 1987).

The implication of this requirement is that a long-term political commitment is needed. The dilemma is that the probable adverse effects of liberalization on employment and income distribution in the short run may render it politically unacceptable and may lead to an "on and off" approach to liberalization and hence to its failure.[2]

The essence of liberalization as defined here is the removal of barriers in all markets of the economy in order to let free-market prices reflect the opportunity costs of resources used in the production process. An interesting aspect of this anti-import-substitution policy is the probability that it may suffer from similar shortcomings. Under import substitution, the infant industry argument has been the initial source of protection of certain domestic industries and assumes that once they reach economies of scale protection will be removed. In practice, however, the perpetual infancy of these industries has led to their perpetual protection, which in turn has partially contributed to the balance of payments crises experienced in the 1970s by the import-substituting countries. Export promotion also calls for incentives to produce exportables and the argument is again an "infant-industry" argument. At the early stages subsidies and other financial and nonfinancial incentives are provided to render the domestic industry, still suffering from the lack of economies of scale, internationally competitive (Khan and Zahler 1987). The prolongation of this period would lead to price distortions and misallocation of resources as it did under import substitution.[3]

A survey of the liberalization literature reveals that there are two issues that the theory has not yet been able to fully address: the timing and sequencing of the liberalization process. Timing refers to the position of the economy along the business cycle at the time liberalization is implemented. It is argued that implementing the policy at a time when the economy is in recession is infeasible because the authorities may within a short time switch their policy stance to place priority on stabilization, which may conflict with liberalization efforts. The speed with which liberalization is implemented is important in terms of the distribution of costs and benefits of policy reforms. Gradual liberalization is favored by those who place importance on the distributional effects of the policy (Michealy 1986). In this respect, the distinction between a gradual as opposed to an abrupt approach to liberalization is in the speed with which relative prices and incomes are altered in the economy. A gradual strategy would spread out the adverse distributional effects of the policy over time. That may prove politically infeasible, however, since at each stage of the liberalization process a new political battle may be necessary. It is further argued that structural rigidities in the economy are the dominant factors in regard to the speed problem. An economy with high rigidities in the labor and capital markets would prefer the gradual approach to allow time for resources to move from low productivity activities to the higher productivity export sector.[4]

The sequence of liberalization refers to the order of markets in the economy to be liberalized. A first-trade-then-capital liberalization scheme is justifiable in terms of the known argument about the speed of adjustment in assets markets, which is presumably faster than that in goods markets. Opening the current account first would initially result in substantial inflows of capital without accomplishing the necessary institutional and structural changes in the economy. Also, the social costs associated with real and portfolio investments cause priority to be given to goods over capital markets, unless investment decisions are guided by shadow prices (Edwards and van Wijnbergen 1987). Opening the capital account first has the advantage of enabling debtor countries to attract foreign capital, thus easing the foreign exchange crisis and the problems associated with debt service.

In terms of domestic markets, liberalization is to be pursued in an inflation-free environment, a dictum of the IMF implying fiscal and monetary discipline to control inflation. A corollary of this dictum is to provide the economic climate for increased savings and investment, both domestic and foreign. However, a limited body of evidence has recently emerged on the role of liberalization of the labor market in the successful implementation of the overall policy. Krueger, for instance, comments: "There is no instance that I know of, however, where a country's trade liberalization has been highly successful in the context of highly restrictive (and enforced) regulations surrounding the labor market" (1978:27).

Krueger also refutes the view held by some that for

liberalization to prove successful real wages need to diminish: "Most successful liberalization appears to have come about not by the removal or reduction in existing wage levels, but rather by a failure to adjust wage levels with future inflation" (1978:28). But quantitative assessment of the role of the labor market in liberalization has yet to be accomplished.

Despite the uncertain theoretical foundations of stabilization-with-liberalization policies, a series of Latin American countries plunged into experimenting with them in the 1970s. Their willingness to try such policies was an outcome of the balance of payments crises in which they found themselves. In the early 1970s a rise in debt burden and a need for additional credit to further development efforts left those nations no choice but to bolster exports in an effort to raise the necessary foreign exchange.

Turkey joined this group for the very same reasons in 1980 with the declaration of the new stabilization-with-liberalization program. The program survived the military takeover of September 12, 1980, the collapse of the informal moneylenders' market at the end of 1981, the election of December 1983, and an alleged "wheelbarrow" money-supply scam in the same year.[5]

The main philosophy of the entire program can be summarized as follows: Using a crawling peg regime and other direct and indirect incentive schemes, the program attempted to shift resources to exports of manufactures. To facilitate this structural change, domestic demand was curbed by means of restrictive policies. Of course, this scheme had substantial effects on the pattern of income distribution in the economy. The apparent priority given to large-scale exporters meant that those who were producing for the domestic economy were made relatively worse off and that small exporters were also adversely affected by the program. Second, the policy package had a major flaw in it in that it contributed to adverse supply developments. In an economy like that of Turkey with no well-developed and regulated financial markets, a squeeze on credit implies that producers must pay a premium on borrowed funds. (In 1987, according to Mr. S. Sabanci, a Turkish businessman, this premium is approximately 30 percent.)[6] In addition, the failure to curb inflation put a burden on fixed income groups. How far the extended family system can survive this repressive situation is open to question. If one takes into consideration the fact that the annual average real wage decrease in manufacturing in the 1982-85 period was 6.9 percent, the adverse distributional effects of the policies become evident.

A COMPARATIVE ASSESSMENT OF TURKISH AND LATIN AMERICAN LIBERALIZATION EXPERIENCES

To gain a comparative perspective, the Turkish liberalization episode is compared and contrasted with those of Chile, Uruguay, and Argentina.[7] All these countries have experimented with economic liberalization of varying magnitudes. Chile started the process in 1974, opening the trade account first. Then Uruguay liberalized the capital account, also in 1974. Argentina followed suit in 1976 by liberalizing the capital account. The initial success of these programs faded by the early 1980s.[8] The behavior of three macroeconomic indicators for selected subperiods is presented in Table 2.1, with the subperiod representing the beginning of the liberalization boxed.

Table 2.1 reveals that in the subperiod preceding the launching of the liberalization policies, low (or negative) output growth and high inflation were common to all countries. Upon the implementation of the new policy, output growth accelerated in Turkey and Uruguay; however, in Argentina and Chile a time lag preceded the rise in output. With respect to inflation, the pattern is uniform. An initial rise in the inflation rate tapers off in the following subperiod and then picks up again in the post-1980 period.

The performance of Turkey, however, differs from that of the Latin American countries. The 1980s mark positive growth and stable (but high) inflation. With regard to unemployment, an increasing pattern is shared by all the countries. In spite of the growth in output, the unemployment rate has not been favorably affected, presumably as a result of a rapid increase in the labor force and the decline in output in import-competing industries, as well as the failure of export-competing industries to absorb this labor surplus in the short run.

An immediate reaction to this discussion may be that Turkish performance in the 1980s compares favorably because the external shocks, the oil price rise and high world interest rates, less adversly affected the Turkish

TABLE 2.1 Comparative Macroeconomic Indicators, 1971-85[a]

	1971-73	1974-76	1977-78	1979-81	1981-83	1984-85
CHILE						
Growth Rate	.7	-2.6	9.0	7.2	-7.4	4.4
Inflation Rate	150.0	364.0	66.0	29.4	18.6	25.3
Unemp. Rate	4.1	13.4	13.8	11.5	18.6	16.9
URUGUAY						
Growth Rate	-.4	4.3	3.3	4.7	-7.7	-.9
Inflation Rate	65.8	69.7	51.4	54.8	34.1	63.8
Unemp. Rate	8.1	10.4	11.0	7.4	13.6	13.5
	1970-72	1973-75	1976-78	1979-80	1981-83	1984-85
ARGENTINA						
Growth Rate	2.7	2.8	.7	3.9	-2.7	-1.0
Inflation Rate	35.6	89.0	265.0	130.2	204.4	649.5
Unemp. Rate	5.8	3.8	3.7	2.2	4.5	4.8
	1970-72	1973-75	1976-77	1978-79	1980-83	1984-85
TURKEY						
Growth Rate	7.8	6.9	7.4	-.2	2.7	5.5
Inflation Rate	11.4	16.8	22.3	52.0	52.7	46.7
Unemp. Rate	13.3	12.6	13.2	13.7	15.5	16.6

Sources: Data on growth and inflation rates are from IMF, *International Financial Statistics*. Unemployment rates for Chile, Uruguay, and Argentina are from ILO, *Labor Statistics Yearbook*. Data for Turkey is from OECD, *Economic Surveys--Turkey*, various issues.

[a]All figures are in average annual percentage changes.

economy than the Latin American economies. A simple calculation of the percentage change in the commodity terms of trade (1978-83 relative to the average of 1975-78), however, shows that the commodity terms of trade deteriorated in Turkey by 28 percent. The figure for Chile was 27 percent. A further calculation shows that the real income effect of the terms of trade change in Turkey, expressed as a percentage of GDP, amounted to -3.05 percent as opposed to Chile's -4.9 percent.[9]

To measure the impact of the rise in the world interest rates in 1979, the nominal and real interest

TABLE 2.2 Fiscal Indicators, 1971-85
(Annual Percentage Change)

	1972-73	1974-76	1977-78	1979-81	1981-83	1984
CHILE						
GDEF/GDP	-10.2	-1.3	-.6	4.3	-1.8	-2.9
GREV/GDP	29.6	30.2	30.7	32.3	28.6	28.9
URUGUAY						
GDEF/GDP	-1.9	-3.4	-1.1	-.5	-6.5	-5.3
GREV/GDP	22.0	20.3	22.6	22.4	21.5	19.2
	1970-72	1973-75	1976-78	1979-80	1981-83	84-85
ARGENTINA						
GDEF/GDP	n.a.	-7.4	-4.4	-3.1	-9.1	n.a.
GREV/GDP	13.3	12.9	14.1	16.9	15.6	n.a.
	1971-72	1973-75	1976-77	1978-79	1980-83	84-85
TURKEY						
GDEF/GDP	-2.6	-1.6	-3.8	-4.6	-3.1	-8.9
GREV/GDP	19.4	18.6	20.5	20.1	20.7	16.6

Sources: IMF, *International Financial Statistics*, various issues.

rates on external debt are calculated for the 1975-78 and 1979-83 periods. In Turkey the nominal interest rate increased from 6.9 percent to 7.9 percent, with the real interest rate jumping from 0.3 percent to 4.0 percent. In Chile, the nominal interest rate rose from 6.0 percent to 9.4 percent, and the real interest rate increased from 0.7 percent to 5.1 percent.[10] Argentina and Uruguay were also susceptible to the rise in interest rates.[11] Thus, the evidence on terms of trade and interest rates rules out the argument that Latin American economies were exposed to stronger external shocks than Turkey was.

An alternative possible source of the difference in macroeconomic performance is each country's domestic stabilization policy. Table 2.2 summarizes the fiscal stance in each country using the central government deficit-GDP ratio (GDEF-GDP). The U-shaped behavior of the GDEF-GDP is striking. As a result of anti-inflationary fiscal policy, the government deficit either in the reform subperiod or in the one immediately following diminishes and then rises due to failure to sustain the low fiscal deficit. In Chile the deficit even turns into a surplus in 1979-81, followed immediately by a severe recession in 1982-83, as shown in Table 2.1. The magnitude of the reduction in the fiscal deficit is much less in Argentina and Turkey than in Uruguay, but there is an initial drop which is followed by an increase.

Two factors seem to have contributed to the eventual rise in fiscal deficits. First, public expenditures in these countries are high due to the presence of and the need for a large public sector. Second, specifically in the 1980s, central government revenues dropped sharply as a result of tax cuts--a measure taken with the expectation of stimulating savings and investment which inadvertently resulted in increased demand. Hence, some argue that excess demand in the 1980s fueled inflation, bringing the countries in our sample back to square one. In the Turkish case, the rise in agricultural support prices may be blamed for the resurgence of the fiscal deficit. But the more one considers the distributional impact of this scheme, the less obvious the adverse effects of the policy become, especially if consideration is given to the fact that more than 45 percent of the labor force is employed in agriculture.[12]

On the monetary side, the experience is not uniform (see Table 2.3). The slowdown in the growth of the nominal money supply (M1) and the negative growth rate of the real money supply, due to the oil price rise, that immediately followed the reform period in Chile and Uruguay was not shared by Argentina. The 1984-85 expansion in the nominal money supply in Argentina was unprecedented. In Turkey, as in Uruguay, money supply growth slowed down, but not enough to curb inflation.

The persistence of high inflation has been a common characteristic in liberalizing economies. As a reaction to this phenomenon, Uruguay, Chile, and Argentina resorted to the use of the exchange rate as an anti-inflationary policy, which resulted in appreciating

TABLE 2.3 Nominal and Real Money Supply Growth, 1970-85
(Annual Average Percentage)

	1970-73	1974-76	1977-78	1979-81	1982-83	1984-85
CHILE						
Nominal	129.4	257.0	119.0	47.7	22.8	18.9[b]
Real[a]	8.6	-106.7	53.0	19.3	-7.2	-15.9[b]
URUGUAY						
Nominal	44.1	64.8	51.5	56.1	13.5	47.9
Real	-7.1	-5.0	.2	1.4	-20.7	-15.9

	1970-72	1973-75	1976-78	1979-80	1981-83	1984-85
ARGENTINA						
Nominal	n.a.	91.7	226.9	138.7	163.3	589.6
Real	n.a.	2.7	-82.8	-28.9	-15.2	-59.8

	1970-72	1973-75	1976-77	1978-79	1980-83	1984-85
TURKEY						
Nominal	20.5	29.0	32.7	44.3	40.0	31.6
Real	8.9	12.2	10.4	-7.7	-12.6	-15.2

Sources: IMF, *International Financial Statistics*, various issues.

[a]Nominal Money Supply Growth - Rate of CPI inflation.

[b]Figures are for 1984.

real exchange rates (see Table 2.4). In Turkey, the real exchange rate has depreciated throughout 1980-85.[13]

As a result of this realistic exchange rate policy to promote exports, the black-market premium on currency, which had reached 6.3 percent in the 1977-79 period, fell to -29.9 percent in 1980-85. (However, how long this undervaluation can be sustained is another matter.)[14] In short, the Turkish exchange rate policy was in accord with the trade liberalization policy, and the conflict between commercial and exchange rate policies observed in Latin American countries was not experienced by Turkey.[15] If this is the case, one would expect that the current account and external debt developments in Turkey would compare favorably with the

TABLE 2.4 Real Exchange Rates, 1973-85[a]
(Annual Percentage Change)

Year	Argentina	Chile	Turkey	Uruguay
1973	n.a.	n.a.	-5.1	-27.8
1974	n.a.	-14.5	-1.7	13.9
1975	n.a.	9.1	2.8	3.9
1976	n.a.	-27.0	4.2	7.9
1977	-4.6	-7.1	2.1	-5.2
1978	-32.6	-5.0	-1.9	-1.0
1979	-31.7	-3.2	-.9	-19.2
1980	-27.7	-14.4	40.4	-16.1
1981	101.4	-4.7	23.8	-1.5
1982	184.9	92.1	19.8	174.4
1983	22.5	5.4	28.2	-10.1
1984	20.2	39.0	20.5	35.0
1985	-34.0	25.0	1.9	11.3

Source: IMF, *International Financial Statistics*, 1986.

[a]Real exchange rate is calculated as (EP*/P), where E is the official exchange rate with P* referring to industrial countries' CPI and P to domestic CPI.

others.

The average current account deficit- (or surplus-) GDP ratios for selected subperiods are given in Table 2.5. A decrease in the ratio either in the period of policy implementation or in the one immediately following it was, in subsequent periods, replaced by an increase (Chile being the exception). In Argentina the ratio even turned positive but eventually bounced back to a deficit. Even though the deficits have been

TABLE 2.5 Current Account--GDP Ratios
(Annual Percentage Change)

	1971-73	1974-76	1977-78	1979-81	1982-83	1984-85
CHILE	-2.9	-2.6	-5.6	-9.1	-7.6	-9.5[a]
URUGUAY	.5	-3.4	-3.2	-.7	-1.8	-2.4
	1971-73	1974-75	1976-78	1979-81	1982-83	1984-85
ARGENTINA	-.3	-1.6	2.1	-2.5	-4.0	n.a.
	1971-73	1974-75	1976-79	1980-83	1984-85	
TURKEY	1.6	-3.3	-4.0	-3.7	-2.8[a]	

Source: IMF, *International Financial Statistics*, 1986.

[a]For 1984 only.

decreasing in Turkey, they are still of considerable magnitude. Turkish figures compared with those of others also show that price competitiveness alone does not boost exports. Factors like quality standards and delivery schedules at times may prove as important as prices (OECD 1986).

Given the low level of domestic savings and current account deficits, resorting to external debt is indeed not surprising. The debt indicators, debt-GNP, debt-export, and debt-service ratios in Table 2.6 indicate that Turkey, like the others, experienced an increase in gross external debt but also, unlike the others, an improvement in the debt-export ratio in 1984 relative to 1981. On the other hand, it maintained a relatively stable debt-service ratio. Even though in relative terms the Turkish debt experience compares favorably with other countries, in absolute terms it has accumulated a considerable debt, totaling 228.3 percent of exports in 1984. A closer look at the structure of debt shows an increasing proportion of short-term debt.

TABLE 2.6 External Debt Indicators

	Debt-GNP ratio[a]		Debt-Export ratio[b]		Debt-Service ratio[c]	
	1981	1984	1981	1984	1981	1984
Argentina	61.2	64.7	285.3	464.0	18.2	29.1
Chile	52.6	115.0	296.2	414.6	29.6	26.2
Turkey	33.1	44.4	324.0	228.3	22.1	22.8
Uruguay	19.3	67.0	117.8	238.9	10.0	29.8

Source: World Bank, World Debt Tables, 1986.

[a]Gross External Debt-GNP.

[b]Gross External Debt-Exports.

[c]Total Debt Servicing-Exports for public and publicly guaranteed debt.

The average maturity of all debts has decreased from 16.1 years in 1980 to 12.2 in 1984 with the grace period dropping from 5 to 3.9 years in the same period, rendering the economy vulnerable to external shocks.[16]

An interesting feature of the stabilization-with-liberalization strategy has become obvious; in the domestic economy inflation and unemployment continue to coexist and external indebtedness rises with variable degrees of debt burden. Also, the cyclical pattern of the variables reviewed here is self-evident. Initial improvement in the subperiod the policies are implemented is generally followed by deterioration in subsequent subperiods. In the literature, various factors have been singled out as the cause of failure of the liberalization programs. Some blame the second oil shock and high world interest rates; others blame inconsistencies in domestic stabilization programs; few blame the conflict between commercial and foreign-exchange policies. Others point to the IMF as the culprit. Probably we have a "Murder on the Orient Express" at hand, where each of these factors has contributed its fair share to the ultimate failure.

CONCLUSIONS

Does the Turkish stabilization-with-liberalization experiment compare favorably with those of Chile, Argentina, and Uruguay? At the outset it must be stressed that the initial inflation, unemployment, and growth rate conditions were in Turkey's favor. Turkey entered the era of liberalization with a history of rapid and high growth and relatively low inflation, not with staggering inflation and a deep recession like Chile, for instance. Hence, the magnitude of the economic malaise was less. Turkey, like Chile and the others, had had the same external shocks. These shocks, in the case of Turkey, hit the economy at the eve of the policy reforms. They affected the other nations after the reforms had been initiated at a time when things started to falter. In Turkey, successful adjustment to the shocks resulted from the commercial and foreign-exchange policies. Real depreciation of the currency and an outward export promotion strategy seem to have kept Turkey ahead of the Southern Cone countries in terms of economic performance. However, domestic stabilization policies to curb inflation and unemployment have failed in Turkey as well as in the other countries. The inability to control fiscal and monetary expansion and, if controlled, to sustain it is a feature shared by all countries in the time period under consideration.

Whether the liberalization strategy has been successful in alleviating the imbalances in the economy needs to be analyzed in due time. However, a limited export base has been founded in Turkey. The continuation and enlargement of it is, unfortunately, a function of politics. It seems that one of the relative advantages Turkey had was the sincere dedication of a (however small) group of politicians to the liberalization program, satisfying the credibility requirement for the successful implementation of the reforms.

In summary, commercial and exchange rate policies are necessary for the successful implementation of a liberalization program. Persistent inflation, unemployment, and increasing indebtedness are the early signals Turkish authorities must recognize from former experience. Unless domestic stabilization is achieved, unless the benefits and costs of export promotion are distributed and shared in an equitable manner, narrowing the current account deficit is not a very meaningful achievement.

NOTES

1. For various definitions of liberalization, see Krueger (1978, 1986), Edwards (1985, 1986), and Corbo and Ossa (1985).

2. Especially in Chile, the high turnover of finance ministers and consequently of policies is one of the many sources of failure of the liberalization policies. See Dornbusch (1984); Calvo (1986).

3. However, for differences in the costs of the two cases, see any development economics textbook.

4. See Feder (1982) for an empirical analysis of the "productivity" argument.

5. See *World Currency Yearbook* (1987:837) for the alleged scam.

6. Milliyet (August 10, 1987). The stagflationary effects of this premium are dealt with in Bruno and Sachs (1985).

7. For a comparison of Turkish and Korean experiences, see Krueger (1987). For a brief discussion of Turkish-Southern Cone countries see Kopits (1987).

8. For a detailed comparison of Latin American and Southeast Asian countries, see Sachs (1985). The main framework of the methodology in this study is based on Sachs' work.

9. The figures on Chile and Argentina are from Sachs. The Turkish figure is calculated using the methodology described in Sachs (1985:517), namely, as the product of percentage change in terms of trade and share of merchandise imports in GDP for 1975-78. The data is from IMF, *International Financial Statistics*.

10. The nominal rate is the implicit rate obtained from the ratio of interest payments to disbursed debt, both long and- medium-term public and publicly guaranteed debt. The real interest rate is the nominal interest rate less the annual rate of change in dollar prices of tradable goods as explained by Sachs (1985:528).

11. Figures for Turkey are calculated using data

from World Bank, *World Debt Tables*, and IMF, *International Financial Statistics*. Figures for Chile are from Sachs (1985).

12. The dilemma is whether one should tailor a country according to the policy or the policy according to the country. The argument par excellence displaying the myopia of international economic relief organizations like IMF, World Bank, and OECD is the U.S. budget deficit and the low inflation rate as argued by Dell (1984). Also note that seigniorage collection to finance government expenditures is common in the countries covered in this study. As Sachs (1985) shows, Latin American countries made extensive use of this method of revenue collection. It is not surprising to find that Turkey frequently resorts to this scheme as well. Calculated as a change in reserve money and GDP ratio, seigniorage collection in Argentina is 10.8, in Chile 2.5, and in Colombia 2.7 percent of GDP in 1975-83 according to Sachs (1985:544). In Turkey our calculations show that the revenues collected by this inflation tax amounted to 3.9 percent of GDP in 1975-83 and 3.5 percent in the 1980-85 period.

13. A theoretically sound measure of real appreciation would refer to real effective exchange rates. As it is, the real exchange rate is expressed in terms of relative inflation. However, the depreciation in the real exchange rate in Turkey in the time period under consideration can be calculated from Kopits (1987:40).

14. The black-market premium is calculated as the difference between the official and black-market rates. The latter is obtained from International Currency Analysis, Inc., *World Currency Yearbook* (1986).

15. For a detailed analysis see Corbo, de Melo, and Tybout (1986).

16. World Debt Tables (1985).

REFERENCES

Bruno, M., and J. Sachs. 1985. *Economics of Worldwide Stagflation.* Cambridge: Harvard University Press.

Calvo, G. A. 1986. Fractured liberalism: Argentina under Martinez de Hoz. *Economic Development and Cultural Change* 3:511-33.

______. 1987. On the costs of temporary liberalization/

stabilization experiments. In *Economic Reform and Liberalization in Latin America*, edited by M. Connolly and C. Gonzales-Vega, 3-17. New York: Praeger.

Cline, W. R. 1982. Can the East Asian model of development be generalized? *World Development* 11:81-90.

Corbo, V., J. de Melo, and J. Tybout. 1986. What went wrong with recent reforms in the Southern Cone? *Economic Development and Cultural Change* 3:606-40.

Corbo, V., and F. Ossa. 1985. Small open economies: The main issues. In *Export-Oriented Development Strategies: The Success of Five Newly Industrializing Countries*, edited by V. Corbo, A. Krueger and F. Ossa, 5-16. Boulder Colo.: Westview Press.

Dell, S. 1984. A note on stabilization and the World Bank. *World Development* 12:165-67.

Dornbusch, R. 1984. Argentina since Martinez de Hoz. National Bureau of Economic Research Working Paper 1466. Cambridge, Mass.: NBER.

Edwards, S. 1985. Stabilization with liberalization: An evaluation of ten years of Chile's experiment with free-market policies, 1973-83. *Economic Development and Cultural Change* 33:223-54.

Edwards, S., and S. van Wijnbergen. 1986. The order of liberalization of the current and capital accounts of the balance of payments. In *Economic Liberalization in Developing Countries*, edited by A. Choksi and D. Papageorgiou, 185-223. New York: Basil Blackwell.

______. 1987. On the appropriate timing and speed of economic liberalization in developing countries. In *Economic Reform and Liberalization in Latin America,* edited by M. Connolly and C. Gonzalez-Vega, 71-92. New York: Praeger.

Feder, G. 1982. On exports and economic growth. *World Bank Staff Paper 508.* Washington, D.C.: The World

Bank.

International Labor Organization. *Labor Statistics Yearbook.* Various issues. Washington, D.C.

International Monetary Fund. *International Financial Statistics.* Various issues. Washington, D. C.: International Monetary Fund.

Khan, M., and R. Zahler. 1987. The liberalization of trade and capital flows in developing countries: Some theoretical and empirical issues. In *Economic Reform and Liberalization in Latin America*, edited by M. Connolly and C. Gonzalez-Vega, 45-67. New York: Praeger.

Kopits, G. 1987. Structural reform, stabilization and growth in Turkey. International Monetary Fund Occasional Paper Series 52. Washington, D.C.: IMF.

Krueger, A. O. 1978. *Liberalization Attempts and Consequences.* New York: NBER.

______. 1985. The experience and lessons of Asia's super exporters. In *Export-Oriented Development Strategies: The Success of Five Newly Industrializing Countries*, edited by V. Corbo, A. Kruger, and F. Ossa, 187-212. Boulder, Colo.: Westview Press.

______. 1987. The importance of economic policy in development: Contrasts between Korea and Turkey. National Bureau of Economic Research Working paper 2195. Cambridge, Mass.: NBER

Michealy, M. 1986. The timing and sequencing of a trade liberalization policy. In *Economic Liberalization in Developing Countries*, edited by A. Choksi and D. Papageorgiou, 41-59. New York: Basil Blackwell.

Organization for Economic Cooperation and Development. *Turkey--Annual Economic Survey.* Various Issues. Paris: OECD.

Sachs, J. 1985. External debt and macroeconomic performance in Latin America and East Asia. *Brookings Papers on Economic Activity* 2:523-64.

3

The Impact of Recent Trade Liberalization Policies in Turkey

PATRICK CONWAY

Developing countries have begun to consider new strategies for maintaining economic growth while reducing trade deficits in goods and nonfactor services. Rising international debt burdens and a growing unwillingness of commercial banks to extend substantial new lending have removed the large trade deficit--the "engine of growth" of the 1970s--from consideration, while maintaining the need to continue debt service payments. Proposals for the engine of the 1980s, often grouped under the rubric "trade liberalization," stem from both dissatisfaction with the record of import-substitution strategies and the importance assigned to market forces by the governments of developed countries. This class of policies includes exchange rate devaluation and tariff and nontariff barrier reduction. Turkey, because it entered its international debt crisis relatively early, has been applying elements of this class of policies since 1980.

Theoretical analyses provide ambiguous conclusions about the impact of these policies on gross domestic product, inflation, economic growth, and the trade balance: Their impact must be evaluated on a country-specific empirical basis. Presented here is an econometric analysis of the Turkish macroeconomy and the impact of its trade liberalization strategy. This analysis suggests that the substantial and continuing exchange rate devaluations of the 1980s considered in isolation served to reduce the trade deficit but at the cost of increasing inflation and reducing output and private investment. Tariff and nontariff barrier reduction in isolation had the opposite effects: Inflation fell, while the trade deficit, output, and investment increased. This reduction can be broken into two parts. Reduction of tariffs on productive inputs will reduce the trade deficit and stimulate output, while the reduction of tariffs on final goods increases the deficit with no significant effect on output or investment.

The first section of this chapter presents an overview of the Turkish policies often referred to as "trade liberalization"; I argue that with respect to imported productive inputs the liberalization strategy began in 1973. The second section is a theoretical statement of the effects of liberalization policies on the small open economy. In the third section I present empirical results that decompose the economic record since 1973 into portions attributable to various government policies. The fourth section offers conclusions and extensions of the results.

THE TURKISH RECORD ON TRADE LIBERALIZATION

Turkey had until 1980 followed a cyclical policy in trade liberalization: Domestic inflation consistently exceeded that of trading partners and caused real appreciation of the exchange rate. Trade liberalization was characterized by infrequent large nominal devaluations coupled with reduced tariffs and nontariff barriers; subsequent real appreciation was accompanied by rising tariffs and nontariff barriers. The 1970s in particular were a period of real appreciation and an inwardly oriented development strategy, culminating in the debt crisis of 1978. By 1979, the government was negotiating with commercial creditors and the International Monetary Fund (IMF) over rescheduling of commercial debt. The economy was burdened with foreign exchange rationing, and a large black market for foreign exchange had burgeoned.

A trade liberalization strategy was introduced in 1980. Its component policies were a large nominal devaluation, reductions in import duties, simplification of import licensing procedures, and credit subsidies to exporters. These positive steps encouraged international observers, leading to an IMF standby agreement, a structural adjustment loan from the World Bank, and a commercial debt rescheduling. In 1981, the government began converting import quotas to import licensing requirements; this process has continued to the present. The Central Bank instituted a policy-variant crawling peg to depreciate the real exchange rate. By 1983, free purchase and sale of foreign exchange had been achieved; in 1984 the import licensing schemes were by law replaced by a progressive tariff system. Concurrently, the government raised interest rates in the domestic financial markets and took steps to reform public enterprises.

The nominal devaluations of the period 1980-84 led to a real depreciation of 74 percent relative to the U.S. dollar. This has been the centerpiece of the liberalization strategy. There was also a large reduction in effective tariff rates, that is, realized government trade tax revenues divided by the value of imports. I separate effective tariffs into petroleum and other to capture differences between tariffs on productive inputs and those on final goods. Table 3.1 lists the evolution of these effective tariff rates over time.

Effective tariff reduction for petroleum products thus began in 1974; other goods benefited from a slight tariff reduction from 1972 through 1975, with rising tariffs thereafter until 1980. The liberalization strategy, as commonly recognized, began in 1980 with large reductions in effective tariffs on both groups of imports.

Nontariff barriers are more difficult to measure directly; I maintain (based upon empirical results discussed below) that in the 1963-80 period nontariff barriers were raised concurrently with effective tariff rates and vice versa.

The liberalization strategy was moderately successful. For the period 1981-84, total exports grew at a 22 percent annual rate in U.S. dollar terms while the imports comparably measured grew at an 8 percent rate. Real gross domestic product (GDP) grew during the same period at a 4.7 percent annual rate. Inflation was substantial during this period, but lower than in the late 1970s; it averaged 35 percent annually as measured by the cost of living index in Ankara.[1] The current account deficit and net foreign borrowing were never eliminated; this is a critical difference between Turkey and debt burdened countries more recently employing

TABLE 3.1 Effective Tariff Rates on Imported Goods[a]

Year	Overall	Petroleum	Other Imports
1972	.42	1.22	.33
1973	.39	1.10	.28
1974	.28	.31	.27
1975	.29	.44	.26
1976	.32	.27	.34
1977	.30	.26	.31
1978	.38	.19	.46
1979	.43	.16	.56
1980	.12	.04	.20
1981	.11	.03	.13
1982	.10	.02	.16
1983	.12	.02	.19
1984	.10	.01	.14

Source: World Bank (1982), Tables 3.3 and 5.2 for 1973-76. SPO (1985) for 1977-83.

[a]The data for petroleum tariffs from 1972-76 are based on total fuel import value except petroleum customs duty and production tax; those after are based on petroleum import value. The earlier period thus understates slightly the effective petroleum tariff.

export-expansion programs.[2] Although the foreign debt crisis continued from 1978 through 1980, the year 1980 stands out as the nadir of recent Turkish experience: 100 percent inflation and negative real GDP growth.

The two major ingredients of the trade liberalization strategy are, then, the real devaluation and the tariff-nontariff barrier reduction. The following section outlines the theoretical impact of these policies on gross domestic product, inflation, investment, and the trade balance.

THE THEORY OF TRADE LIBERALIZATION

The gains from trade liberalization have traditionally been couched in partial-equilibrium terms; McKinnon (1973) and Balassa (1982) stress the efficiency gains from such policies. The first general-equilibrium, or macroeconomic, analyses of the liberalization strategy focused on the role of the exchange rate. Authors beginning with Robinson (1947) introduced Keynesian effects on domestic income and output into partial-equilibrium trade models. The Marshall-Lerner condition for devaluation to improve the trade balance was confirmed in that case as well. In the strict Keynesian formulation, the aggregate price level remains unchanged. The "absorption analysis" of Alexander (1952) restates these conclusions in terms of the relation of the trade balance of domestic income and expenditure.

More recently, authors have presented plausible theoretical explanations for contractionary effects of devaluation on output. Cooper (1971) suggests a number of reasons that devaluation might contract domestic expenditure: revaluation of foreign debt, a credit squeeze due to a smaller real money supply, induced speculative spending prior to the devaluation, and the efficiency losses due to distortionary effects on expenditure decisions. Krugman and Taylor (1978) suggest that weak export response to devaluation could lead to output contraction.

The first overlay to this view of the open economy was due to Salter (1959) and Swan (1963). Their "dependent economy" model extended the previous analysis to include both traded and nontraded goods, while restricting their discussion to the "small" economy--one with no influence over international prices of traded goods.[3] This framework has suggested a reassessment of the impact of trade liberalization; Buffie (1984) demonstrates that nontraded sector losses from trade liberalization can offset the traded-sector gains.

The fluctuations in international imported-input prices in the 1970s triggered economic research on the role of such inputs in the trade balance and the domestic economy. This research focused on imported inputs as determinants of aggregate supply; the infinite export and import supply elasticities of the earlier Keynesian models were replaced with production-function relationships of output to productive inputs. Bruno and Sachs (1979), for example, examined three-factor (capital, labor, energy) functions. Conway (1987) summarizes the work in this area.

Imported inputs affect the trade balance in two ways: directly as imports, and indirectly as their cost reduces domestic income. This introduces two new channels for the impact of devaluation and trade liberalization. Findlay and Rodriguez (1977) pointed out the output-reducing effect of increased energy prices in an open economy with imported energy input and no access to international credit.[4] Other authors have followed this path; Bruno and Sachs (1985) provide a summary of that work. Devaluation can cause an increased relative price of imported inputs in nontraded sectors and lead to a movement toward trade deficit, lower domestic product, and increased price level. Reduction of tariffs on imported inputs will have the opposite effect.

Contractionary devaluation due to the importance of imported inputs has been discussed by Taylor (1983), Conway (1986), and van Wijnbergen (1986), among others. The Marshall-Lerner condition may hold for exogenous income levels; with endogenous domestic income, however, the negative impact of the devaluation on supply-side factors may outweigh the positive demand-side stimulus. The domestic price level rises unambiguously in this case, and there is movement toward trade deficit.[5]

I have incorporated each of these overlays into a theoretical macroeconomic model of an open economy. Table 3.2 states the comparative static results of various temporary "trade liberalization" policies. The goals are the trade balance (B), gross domestic product (y), private investment (IP) and inflation (π). Policy components are nominal devaluation (r), final-good tariff reduction (t_f), and imported-input tariff reduction (t_m).

The striking aspects are (1) the ambiguity of the impact of devaluation on the macroeconomic goals and (2) the opposing nature of many of these policies. The more recent overlays of the theory have provided a number of reasons for the trade balance and GDP to react in perverse ways to liberalization policies.

The effects of permanent liberalizing changes can be derived in similar fashion in intertemporal models of decision making. All policies then have ambiguous effects on the trade balance, as present consumption and private investment are both stimulated by expected future gains.

There are three crucial elements for resolving the ambiguous effects of devaluation that relate to the overlays of traditional theory. The first is the degree to which domestic (nontraded) prices are independent of international prices; the more aggregate prices of final

TABLE 3.2 The Impact of Short-Run Trade Stabilization and Liberalization Policies

Endogenous Variable	The Stabilizing/Liberalizing Change in		
	r	t_f	t_m
B	?	?	+
y	?	-	+
IP	?	-	+
π	+	-	0

goods rise with devaluation, the more positive the impact on output and the trade balance. The second is the direction and degree of exchange rate responsiveness of consumption and private investment spending; if it has a negative effect, greater responsiveness leads to greater positive impact on the trade balance. The third is the size and own-price responsiveness of demand for imported productive inputs; the smaller the size and the lower the price responsiveness, the more positive the impact on output and the trade balance.

TRADE LIBERALIZATION: EMPIRICAL RESULTS

Table 3.3 presents a simple macroeconomic model for Turkey based upon the absorption approach to the balance of payments. The parameters were estimated with data from Turkish sources for the period 1963-83.[6] The inflation equation is estimated as a reduced form; the other equations form a simultaneous system, with estimation done through two-stage least squares. T-statistics are presented in parentheses and R^2 is adjusted for degrees of freedom. The estimates of aggregate productive relationships clearly capture the importance of imported intermediate inputs in production. The own-price elasticity of demand for these inputs is -1.06 and is statistically indistinguishable from unity (but statistically different from zero at the 95 percent level of confidence).

Tariffs on these inputs enter separately in the imported-input demand equation and have a point elas-

TABLE 3.3 Macroeconomic Model for Turkey: Estimation for the Period 1963-84

1) $$\ln Q_s = .92 \ln y_s + 0.8 \ln E_s + .0002s \qquad R^2 = 1.00$$
(139.95) (16.30) $\qquad DW = 1.32$

2) $$\ln y_s = -.19D + .67 \ln K_s + .18 \ln L_s + .15 \ln E_s + .0002s \qquad R^2 = 1.00$$
(60.5) (16.84) (6.59) (2.45) $\qquad DW = 1.48$

3) $$\ln L_s = 1.7 - .06 \ln Q_s + .21 \ln K_s + .04 \ln \omega_s \qquad R^2 = .99$$
(52.43) (1.61) (5.81) (3.28) $\qquad DW = 1.91$

4) $$\ln E_s = -2.93 + 1.20 \ln Q_s - 1.06 \ln(r_s q_s^* / P_s) - 3.92 \ln(1+t_s) \qquad R^2 = .99$$
(5.62) (12.19) (5.60) (10.05) $\qquad DW = 1.72$

5) $$\ln RC_s = .24 + .93 \ln y_s + .02 \ln e_s - .23 \ln(1+t_s) - .09\, \mathfrak{r}_s \qquad R^2 = 1.00$$
(1.51) (33.84) (0.38) (2.99) (0.97) $\qquad DW = 1.52$

6) $$\ln P_{ks} IP_s = -2.13 + 1.27 \ln y_s + .03 \ln e_s - 1.42\, \mathfrak{r}_s \qquad R^2 = .94$$
(5.61) (15.97) (0.15) (3.33) $\qquad DW = 2.10$

7) $$\ln (MS_s / P_s) = .02 - 1.92 R_s - .07 \pi_s^e + 1.17 \ln y_s \qquad R^2 = .95$$
(0.08) (7.47) (0.69) (12.84) $\qquad DW = .87$

8) $$\ln (BO_s / P_s) = -3.31 + 2.32 R_s + .67 \ln y_s - .59 \pi_s^e \qquad R^2 = .75$$
(4.07) (3.40) (2.77) (2.13) $\qquad DW = 1.11$

9) $$B_s = y_s - RC_s - P_{ks} IP_s - IG_s - G_s + ADJ_s$$

---

10) $$\pi = -.12 + 1.32\pi^* + .31(\hat{q^*/P^*}) + .48\hat{r} + .64(1+\hat{t}_m) + .54\hat{MS} \qquad R^2 = .94$$
(2.42) (1.81) (2.56) (4.01) (1.38) (2.65) $\qquad DW = 1.78$

K = real capital stock
$P_k IP$ = real value of private investment(+)
y = real gross domestic product(+)
E = real imported input use(+)
q^*/P^* = real \$ price of imported inputs
P = aggregate price index(+)
P^* = US GDP deflator
t = effective tariff on imported goods
P_k/P = real \$ capital-good price
MS = nominal money supply
R = nominal domestic interest rate
π^e = expected inflation
D = dummy: 1 in 1980-84, zero otherwise

IG = real government investment
Q = total output(+)
L = labor use(+)
ω = real wage
e = real wage
ADJ = real indirect - real stock changes
G = real government expenditure
r = nominal exchange rate
$\mathfrak{r}$ = real international rate of return
BO = quasi-money supply(+)
RC = real private consumption(+)
B = balance of trade(+)
(+)indicates an endogenous variable

ticity of -3.92. This figure, significantly larger in absolute value than the own-price elasticity, suggests that tariff and nontariff barriers were raised and lowered concurrently. The estimated total value share of imported inputs in gross output is .22, clearly a sizable contribution. Trade liberalization policies will then be contractionary to the extent that they raise the domestic cost of imported inputs and expansionary to the extent that they lower the cost.

The dummy variable introduced for the period 1980-83 is significantly smaller than one; this indicates a reduction in GDP of 17 percent below potential during these years. Trade liberalization should in theory increase productive efficiency, not decrease it. These estimates may reflect the temporary misallocation of resources during adjustment to the sweeping reforms of the 1980s or non-economic factors related to civil unrest and military intervention. The dummy technique is a strictly statistical procedure; our understanding will be improved through research into the underlying causes of that shift.

Estimation suggests that trade liberalization policies will also have an impact on the expenditure side. Private consumption and investment decisions are slightly encouraged by real devaluation, although the coefficients in both cases are insignificantly different from zero. Tariff and nontariff barrier reduction on final goods increases private consumption, thus worsening the trade balance.[7] The expenditure functions have a textbook form, with current GDP as a determinant. Estimation demonstrated a close tie between private expenditure and GDP, with a calculated marginal propensity to spend on consumption and private investment in 1980 of 87 percent. Expenditure also reacts negatively to increases in the real interest rate. The international and domestic rates have moved in tandem (with a correlation coefficient of .71), and the international rate provided the better explanatory power. Changes in $\Re_s$ have large significant effects on private investment and play a large role in the following simulations in explaining the recent slowdown in private investment.[8]

The reduced-form estimation in equation 10 allows rejection of the hypothesis of complete domestic price determination by international prices: Nominal devaluations do cause real depreciation, as the earlier evidence indicated. This implies as well that the

TABLE 3.4 Outlier Analysis for y_s Predictions

Year	Percent Deviation from Data
1973	-0.8[a]
1974	-0.1
1975	1.9
1976	2.1
1977	-2.5
1978	-0.3
1979	-2.8
1980	1.2
1981	-1.4
1982	-0.7
1983	1.6
1984	5.3

[a]Negative entry indicates historical GDP exceeded forecast GDP.

production cost-increasing impact of devaluation may have contractionary effects on output, while imported-input tariff liberalization may have disproportionately large output expansion effects.

Dynamic simulation analysis with the model of Table 3.3 demonstrates the magnitude of effects of government policy shifts on the Turkish trade account, output, private investment, and the price level.[9] It thus provides a quantification of the "comparative statics" effects summarized in Table 3.2. The simulations of the inflation equation are conducted independently of production and expenditure equations. The model predicts very well for the sample period, as the R^2 of the estimation equations in Table 3.3 would suggest. Table 3.4 indicates the deviation of simulated gross domestic product from the historical value. The model is thus quite accurate for in-sample predictions; although true for all variables, the financial-sector equations provide a less satisfying fit.

Decompositions of the impact of the government's policies on the trade balance, gross national product,

TABLE 3.5 Decomposition of Gross Domestic Product (y), 1973-84[a]

	Percentage Change in y_s Due to		
Time Period	dr	dt_m	dt_f
1973-77	4.9	8.1	0.0
1978-79	7.8	4.1	0.0
1980-84	-3.2	20.0	0.0
1973-84	1.7	12.9	0.0

[a]Averages formed by summing across all observations of impact for time period and dividing by summed historical GDP for the same period.

private investment (as an indicator of future economic growth), and inflation are presented through successive simulations of the model. Each simulation is a comparative static exercise, with the time series of the policy under consideration changed in simulation to "base" values forecast for the 1974-84 period by autoregression of the variable on pre-1973 data. The change in equilibrium values of endogenous variables then indicates the impact of that policy, ceteris paribus.

During the post-1973 period, the real exchange rate was appreciated relative to base during 1973-79 and depreciated relative to base for the liberalization period. For a base value comparison of the actual nominal exchange rate strategy, the exchange rate is fixed at 1972 levels, inflation occurs at the world (here proxied by U.S.) inflation rate for 1973-84, and the money supply grows to maintain a fixed domestic interest rate. Base values for tariffs are derived from pre-1973 trends. Tariffs on final goods and productive inputs dropped during the liberalization period and were much reduced at that time from the base.[10]

The impact of policy changes on gross domestic product is presented in Table 3.5. The impact of devaluation in isolation is further evidence of a

TABLE 3.6 Decomposition of the Value of Private Investment ($P_{ks}IP_s$), 1973-84[a]

Time Period	Percentage Change in $P_{ks}IP_s$ Due to		
	dr	dt_m	dt_f
1973 - 77	17.2	10.2	0.0
1978 - 79	12.7	5.2	0.0
1980 - 84	-27.1	24.8	0.0
1973 - 84	- 0.6	14.8	0.0

[a]Averages formed by summing across all observations of impact for time period and dividing by summed private investment value for the same period.

Turkish "contractionary devaluation" phenomenon, as discussed in the theoretical literature by Taylor (1983) and van Wijnbergen (1986) and for Turkey in Conway (1986). The period of appreciation led to increases between 5 and 8 percent in GDP; the depreciation of the liberalization period had a negative impact equal to 3.2 percent of GDP.

The reduction in tariffs and nontariff barriers to imported inputs was expansionary; in the 1970s, this already had an impact within the range of 3 to 8 percent of GDP. In the liberalization period, the positive effect on GDP was even more striking; GDP was forecast to rise by 20 percent, ceteris paribus, through this policy change alone. Tariff reduction on final goods did not affect gross domestic product, although it had a large effect on private consumption and the trade balance.

Table 3.6 illustrates the impact of these policies on the value of private investment decisions. The value of private investment (i.e., the volume of investment times the relative domestic price of capital) provides an indication of future economic growth opportunities stimulated by the trade liberalization policy. Simulation results indicate that the devaluation policy of

TABLE 3.7 Decomposition of Turkish Trade Balance (B), 1973-84[a]

Time Period	Percent Change in B_s Due to		
	dr	dt_m	dt_t
1973 - 77	-11.3	7.0	-17.7
1978 - 79	5.7	3.0	- 5.1
1980 - 84	25.3	29.2	-51.2
1973 - 84	7.5	14.5	-27.2

[a]Averages formed by summing across all observations of impact for time period and dividing by summed B for the same period. Negative entry indicates increased deficit.

1980-84 discouraged private investment relative to the base trend. Although the domestic price of capital rises with devaluation, the volume of investment falls by more and leads to a large negative decline. Influenced somewhat by the increase in the real exchange rate, it is largely the result of an increased real interest rate brought about by continuing devaluation and the contractionary effect of devaluation on gross domestic product. Devaluation implies that unchanging foreign-currency liabilities will require continually more domestic currency to finance. If the market for output remains predominantly a domestic one, devaluation will discourage investment.[11] Final-good tariffs, on the other hand, were found to have no effect on private investment.

Imported-input tariff liberalization, to the extent that it expanded output, also expanded private investment: The positive effect of this totaled 24.8 percent of private investment value, ceteris paribus, in the liberalization period.

Table 3.7 presents the impact of these liberalization policies on the trade balance. The policy of devaluation is estimated to have reduced the trade deficit. The 1970s were a period of real appreciation;

TABLE 3.8 Decomposition Results: Inflation Rate[a]

Time Period	The Percent Contribution of				
	q^*	r	t	MS	π^*
1973 - 77	25.1	2.2	-1.8	48.5	26.0
1978 - 79	15.5	24.8	7.1	36.1	16.5
1980 - 84	- 4.1	63.2	-3.5	31.7	12.7
1973 - 84	7.8	39.0	-0.6	37.0	16.8

[a]Averages formed by summing across all observations of impact for time period and dividing by summed historical inflation rates for the same period.

the exchange rate policy ceteris paribus also led to increases in the trade deficit.[12] The real depreciation of the 1980s similarly caused a reduction in the deficit. The trade liberalization policy with the greatest positive impact on the trade balance, however, was the lowering of tariffs and nontariff barriers on productive inputs. Liberalization of tariffs on final goods contributed strongly to the continued trade deficit.

International inflation has contributed significantly to Turkish inflation in all periods, as indicated by the impact of international final-good (P*) and imported-input (q*) prices (see Table 3.8). Money supply growth has also been important, although it had its greatest relative impact during the expansionary 1973-77 period. Exchange rate devaluation also contributed heavily to the inflation rate; its average for the entire period was 39.0 percent of total inflation and reflects both increases in final-good prices and the increase in the domestic-currency price of imported inputs. The reduction in tariff rates (final-good and input tariffs are taken together here) was deflationary on average, although its impact was small.

The impact of the trade liberalization strategy is

captured in the summary row for 1980-84, and accords well with the theoretical predictions of Table 3.2. The devaluations of the period led to increased inflation and accounted for well over half the average inflation for the period. Tariff reduction lowered prices through lower production costs and through lower imported final-good prices. The fall in the U.S. dollar price of imported inputs reduced inflation, while U.S. dollar final-good price inflation raised it somewhat.

CONCLUSIONS, QUALIFICATIONS, AND EXTENSIONS

The estimations and simulations reported in this chapter call into question an excessive reliance on nominal devaluation for achieving both short-run trade balance goals and long-run economic growth goals. Devaluations are effective in reducing the trade deficit, but this effectiveness appears to occur through investment reduction rather than expenditure switching to domestic goods. The result is lower output levels through higher costs of productive inputs and lower economic growth rates through reduced private investment. There is also a large inflation cost from the policy.

Reduction of tariffs on productive inputs has salutary effects on all variables, mainly through its encouragement of production. Reduction of tariffs on final goods seems predominantly to expand private consumption; it had an insignificant impact on investment decisions and production. The insight afforded by the absorption approach used here is that a liberalization policy effective in reducing the trade deficit will increase domestic production by more than any increase in expenditure. Turkish evidence suggests that devaluation by itself may lower GDP by increasing production costs; its effectiveness is due to reducing private investment by even more. Preferable policies will be those that stimulate production (as in reducing tariffs on imported inputs) or reduce less vital categories of expenditure.

These results differ from previous research for both modeling and data reasons. In Conway (1986; 1987, Ch. 7) I conclude that devaluation was inflationary and output reducing; I also find, contrary to the results reported in this chapter, that it may have worsened the trade deficit. The estimation period differs slightly, with the present chapter having three additional years of data. This chapter also uses a simpler formulation of private consumption and investment behavior. In place of a separation of private actors into capital owners and labor and a modeling of the intertemporal decisionmaking of the former, I use the traditional macroeconomic functions that assign a large role to present GDP for determining present expenditure. Also in this chapter, as opposed to previous work, the impact of devaluation on the real interest rate on international borrowing is incorporated--this has a large negative effect on private investment, thus reducing expenditure. This chapter's formulation is less well grounded in microeconomic foundations but explains expenditure behavior well in sample and provides a sensitivity analysis for earlier results.[13] The two specifications differ only in their prediction of devaluation's impact on the trade deficit; in other policy evaluations they are qualitatively the same.

The Turkish record can serve as an example for other debt-burdened countries. A trade liberalization prescription should be examined component by component before adoption; nominal devaluations may be counter-productive components of such a prescription. There is also a strong indication in these results that the dominant impact from trade liberalization came through lower-cost access to imported productive inputs. There is a traditional presumption that liberalization will have its major impact on the final-good market, with any effect on the production process secondary. These results suggest the reverse: If only one form of trade liberalization is possible, a country with Turkey's characteristics and import-substitution heritage may well find that imported-input liberalization should have priority.

This analysis is only as strong as the data on which it is based. Turkish data series are complete, but often revised; the most recent revision was in 1984, and those data are incorporated here. There is also no natural distinction in the data between tariff receipts from imported inputs and from final goods. As a result, an aggregate effective tariff series is used and makes the distinction in estimation and simulation between the two types of tariffs only approximate. The conclusions are also model dependent. Proponents of liberalization often tout its "X-efficiency" gains; these would appear through an outward shift in the productive technology. They are only modeled here in the GDP function and lead to an inward shift in empirical estimation through 1983. The issue, however, deserves more detailed sectoral analysis before firm conclusions are drawn. Finally, there is no discussion of income distributional issues. Conway (1987) treats this issue in more detail; there is some evidence (Celasun 1986) that the size distribution of income has worsened in the liberalization period.

NOTES

1. The year 1980 serves as the base for these calculations; it should be noted that 1980 is historically below trend for output and above trend for inflation and imports.

2. The trade deficit for goods and nonfactor services was 5 percent of GDP in 1978; by 1984 it was 6 percent. The difference was financed through remittances and through net foreign borrowing.

3. The term "dependent economy" is used by Dornbusch (1980, ch. 6) in his excellent exposition of the Salter-Swan paradigm. Given the assumptions of the dependent economy model, exports and imports can be aggregated into a single traded good.

4. For simplicity they specify the production function to be Leontief in inputs: This provides the impact in the limit of zero factoral substitutability in production.

5. The most recent overlay of the open-economy model has been the incorporation of intertemporal decisionmaking and international credit markets in domestic expenditure behavior. The theoretical literature on decisionmaking over two periods, as represented by Marion and Svensson (1984), Sachs (1981), Svensson and Razin (1983), van Wijnbergen (1984), and Conway (1986) introduces optimal intertemporal expenditures by a representative individual. In this framework, the perceived permanence of the liberalization strategy determines its effect on the economy. Real devaluation and tariff reduction can then have opposing intertemporal expenditure-switching effects: Temporary real devaluation can lead to a reduction in present consumption and investment, while temporary final-good tariff reduction can cause increased present consumption. Permanent devaluation and tariff reduction

would not have these switching effects, although any gains in income due to the policies would be "smoothed" across a number of periods.

6. Conway (1987) presents a detailed description of the data used in this estimation and the methodology used in estimation and simulation. The present model differs from that one because of its exclusion of intertemporal decisionmaking, its inclusion of money and domestic bond markets, its aggregation of private wage-earners into a single group, and its neglect of the determinants of government decisionmaking.

7. Tariffs played an insignificant role in the investment equation. This perhaps reflects the absence of tariff and nontariff barriers to imports during this period in Turkey.

8. The investment value response to real international interest rates is larger than in Conway (1986, 1987); this could be due to $\Re$'s correlation with variables omitted from this equation (e.g., the price of capital goods).

9. These are static simulations in the sense that the capital stock is not updated using endogenously generated values of investment. Conway (1987) uses a dynamic simulation technique.

10. Similar base values were formed and simulations run for the exogenous real international interest rate, real wage, and imported productive input price. The real imported-input price in dollar terms lay above base values during the entire period, with its value reapproaching base during 1984. The real international interest rate fell below base during the period 1973-79 and rose above base for the 1980s. The real wage during the 1970s remained above base but dropped sharply below during the liberalization phase. The results of simulation are not presented but are available from the author upon request.

11. If the firm's product is marketed internationally, this continuing devaluation need not discourage investment. This is thus one area where the conclusions of the simulation based predominantly on the inward-oriented pre-1980 period may be misleading for the outward-oriented post-1980 years.

12. Cf. Conway (1986). The difference in the results reported here is due to (1) the liquidity-constrained nature of private consumption and investment behavior and (2) the addition that devaluation raises

the real interest rate on foreign borrowing. The former ensured that current output reductions led to expenditure reductions as well. The latter induced a large private investment response.

13. It does, however, understate the impact of external shocks on the trade deficit. While Balassa (1982) and Conway (1986) find comparable deficitary impacts of the real oil price increase of the 1970s of 6-7 percent of GDP, the present model predicts a movement toward deficit of only about 1 percent of GDP. The difference is due to the GDP-dependent specification of the expenditure equations.

REFERENCES

Alexander, S. 1952. Effects of a devaluation on a trade balance. *IMF Staff Papers* 2:263-78.

Balassa, B. 1982. *Development Strategies in Semi-Industrial Economies*. Baltimore: Johns Hopkins Press.

Bruno, M., and J. Sachs. 1979. Macro-economic adjustment with import price shocks: Real and monetary aspects. National Bureau of Economic Research Working Paper 340. Cambridge, Mass.:NBER.

______. 1985. *Economics of Worldwide Stagflation*. Cambridge: Harvard University Press.

Buffie, E. 1984. Macroeconomics of trade liberalization. *Journal of International Economics* 17:121-37.

Celasun, M. 1986. Income distribution and domestic terms of trade in Turkey, 1978-1983. *METU Studies in Development 13* (1-2):193-216.

Conway, P. 1986. Decomposing the determinants of trade deficits: Turkey in the 1970s. *Journal of Development Economics* 22:235-58.

______. 1987. *Economic Shocks and Structural Adjustments: Turkey after 1973*. Amsterdam: North Holland.

Cooper, R. 1971. Currency devaluation in developing countries. *Princeton Essays in International*

Finance 86:3-31.

Dornbusch, R. 1980. *Open-Economy Macroeconomics.* New York: Basic Books.

Findlay, R., and C. Rodriguez. 1977. Intermediate imports and macroeconomic policy under flexible exchange rates. *Canadian Journal of Economics* 10:208-17.

Krugman, P., and L. Taylor. 1978. Contractionary effects of devaluation. *Journal of International Economics* 8:445-56.

Marion, N., and L. Svensson. 1984. World equilibrium and oil price: An intertemporal analysis. *Oxford Economic Papers* 36(1):86-102.

McKinnon, R. I. 1973. *Money and Capital in Economic Development.* Washington, D.C.: The Brookings Institution.

Robinson, J. 1947. *Essays in the Theory of Unemployment.* Oxford: Blackwell.

Sachs, J. 1981. The current account and macroeconomic adjustment in the 1970s. *Brookings Papers on Economic Activity* 1:201-68.

Salter, W. 1959. Internal and external balance: The role of price and expenditure effects. *Economic Record* 35(71):226-38.

Svensson, L., and A. Razin. 1983. The terms of trade and the current account: The Harberger-Laursen-Metzler effect. *Journal of Political Economy* 91(1):97-125.

Swan, T. 1963. Longer-run problems of the balance of payments. In *The Australian Economy*, edited by H. Arndt and W. Corden, 349-95. Melbourne: Cheshire Press.

Taylor, L. 1983. *Structuralist Macroeconomics: Applicable Models for the Third World.* New York: Basic Books.

van Wijnbergen, S. 1984. The optimal investment and current account response to oil price shocks under putty-clay technology. *Journal of International Economics* 17: 138-47.

______. 1986. Exchange rate management and stabilization policies in developing countries. *Journal of Development Economics* 23:227-47.

4

Exchange Rate Liberalization and Economic Stability: The Turkish Experience

M. ERCAN KUMCU

With the emergence of international payments crises in some developing countries, economic growth with price stability has once again become a popular issue. One distinguishing feature of countries with external payments problems is the existence of significant public sector fiscal deficits which arise from ambitious social and economic programs. Central banks in such countries lack well-developed financial markets and have little control over the money supply. Since neither fiscal discipline by the public sector nor money supply control by the central banks is likely to occur, the burden of adjustment in these countries consequently falls on private savings, which require realistic real exchange rate and real interest rate policies.

This chapter focuses on the role of real exchange rate and real interest rate policies in stabilization programs with reference to the Turkish experience during the last decade. The first part develops a short-term model of the economy in line with the Mundell-Fleming approach.[1] The model assumes producers' output response to always be profit maximizing and allows the domestic country to run a current account deficit only to the extent that the rest of the world permits. It also assumes the labor market does not clear instantaneously while the money supply is endogenous, the foreign borrowing constraint is always binding, and an excess demand for final output always prevails. A similar model is presented in Saracoglu (1985). A Phillips curve relationship derived from such a model is upward sloping. Accordingly, the adverse effects of declining foreign borrowing can be prevented as long as the domestic currency is allowed to depreciate in real terms and the real interest rate is raised. In this short-run model, a depreciating domestic currency in real terms, as well as a rising real rate of interest, will stimulate output growth while reducing domestic prices.

In the second part of the analysis, the response of output growth and inflation to real exchange rate and real interest rate policies is tested empirically in a vector autoregression framework, using Turkish data from 1975 to 1985. Empirical results indicate that the Turkish experience with real exchange rates and real interest rate policies is consistent with the predictions of the model.

THE MODEL

Consider a small domestic economy with a single good y, which is exported as well as domestically consumed, and a single commodity import M, which is used in the production of y as well as consumed domestically as a final good. The production function of the domestically produced good has the twin properties of constant returns to scale and homotheticity defined over labor and the imported intermediate product, which is also a perfect substitute for the imported consumption good.[2]

The supply of exports is assumed to depend on the relative prices of the foreign good with respect to the domestic good such that

$$X = X(ep^*/p) = X(q) \quad ; \quad X'>0, \qquad (4.1)$$

where X is real exports, p is the domestic price level, e is the exchange rate (the domestic price of foreign currency), p* is the foreign price level, and q is the real exchange rate. The small country assumption implies that the demand for exports is infinitely elastic; thus the supply of exports determines the level of equilibrium exports.

Total imports, M, both for consumption and intermediate use (N), are assumed to be a function of domestic income, the real exchange rate, and the real interest rate. The real interest rate is an argument of this function because of its impact on the consumption of both domestically produced and imported goods.

$$M = M(y,q,r) \quad ; \quad M_y>0,\ M_q<0,\ \text{and}\ M_r<0, \qquad (4.2)$$

where y is domestic real income (output), and r is the real interest rate. The impact of the real interest rate on imports is negative because the real interest rate positively affects savings and thus reduces the consumption of both domestically produced and imported goods.

The domestic product, y, is produced by a constant return to scale, homothetic technology such that

$$y = F(N/L)L \quad ; \quad F'>0, \qquad (4.3)$$

where N is the imported intermediate product and L is the labor input. The homotheticity of the production function implies that the ratio of input quantities is a function of the ratio of input prices. While this assumption is by no means necessary for our conclusions, it simplifies the exposition. Hence, equation (4.3) can be rewritten as

$$y = f(w/ep^*)L = f[(w/p)/q]L \quad ; \quad f'>0, \qquad (4.4)$$

where w is the nominal wage rate in the domestic country. Note that output is an increasing function of the real wage, a result that needs some further explanation. At a given level of employment, a profit-maximizing producer will choose an imported input level where the isocost line is tangent to the isoquant curve at the given level of output as shown in Figure 4.1. At output level y_1, the levels of labor and imported input employment will be L_1 and N_1, respectively. An increase in real wages would make the imported input relatively less expensive. When labor is kept at L_1, the profit-maximizing producer responds by increasing the use of the imported input to a level at which a relatively less steep isocost becomes tangent to a higher isoquant curve. As shown in Figure 4.1, the use of the imported input will be at N_2 when output expands to y_2 at the initial level of labor L_1.

In what follows, we assume that the domestic country is facing a binding foreign borrowing constraint. The foreign borrowing is exogenous and is determined by

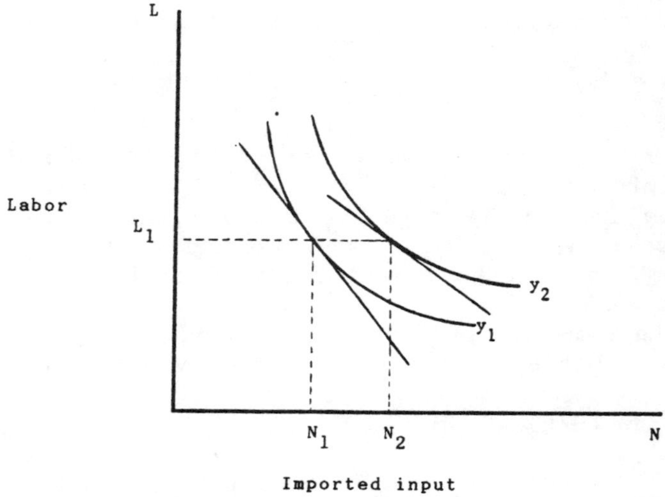

Figure 4.1. Imported input-labor ratios at a given employment level.

the rest of the world, such that

$$M(y,q,r) - (1/q)X(q) = B, \quad (4.5)$$

where B is the current account deficit measured in real terms in units of the foreign good.[3]

The money supply in this model is endogenous. The demand for money can be approximated by a classical transactions equation

$$m/p = k(q,r)\ y, \quad (4.6)$$

where m is the nominal money supply and k is the inverse of the transactions velocity of money. As the real exchange rate and the real interest rate are taken to be policy variables, and real output and domestic prices are determined by equations (4.4) and (4.5), the domestic money supply in equation (4.6) will be endogenous for a money market equilibrium.

Provided that the Marshall-Lerner condition holds,[4] equation (4.5) will combine a real output and a real exchange rate at a given rate of real interest, satisfying the foreign borrowing constraint. This implies that a depreciating domestic currency will be consistent with a higher domestic production level as

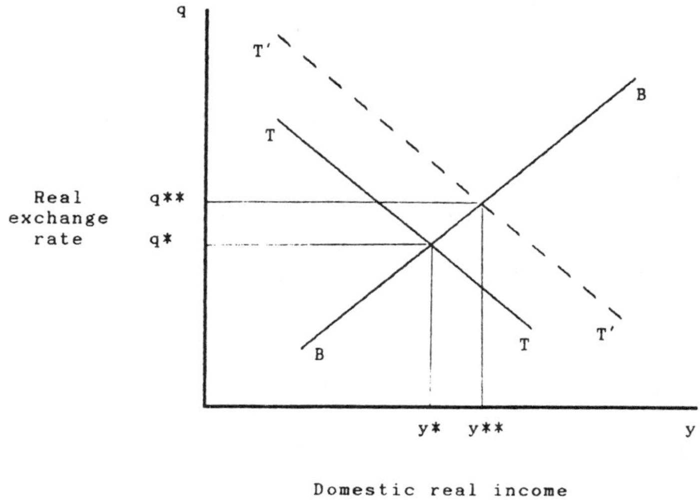

Figure 4.2. Effect of real exchange rate depreciation on output.

shown by the BB line in Figure 4.2.

In the very short run, labor input level and nominal wages are assumed fixed as in Brito and Richardson (1975). This assumption implies that any adjustment in production will result from change in the relative prices of inputs, the real exchange rate, or the domestic price level.[5] Thus, as follows from equation (4.4) and shown by the TT line in Figure 4.2, the appreciation of domestic currency will be associated with higher real output.

The real exchange rate and real interest rate levels set by the government are also consistent with the level of domestic prices and real output. For example, if the government sets a real exchange rate level above q* in Figure 4.2, exports will increase and imports will decline, resulting in a lower current account deficit if the Marshall-Lerner condition holds. Under a binding foreign borrowing constraint, the domestic country would be able to increase imports at the same real exchange rate level with a higher level of output. However, for real output to rise at a given level of labor input, producers would have to use more of the imported input, which would only be possible with profit-maximizing behavior, if labor becomes relatively more expensive. This implies that real wages must increase through lower domestic prices shifting the TT line to T′T′. In short, this simple model produces an inverse Phillips curve between prices and output, generated by a real depreciation or appreciation of the domestic currency.[6]

A similar Phillips curve can also occur with a real interest rate policy. Suppose that the government raises the real interest rate, thereby reducing the demand for imports and lowering the current account deficit. Under a binding foreign borrowing constraint, the current account deficit level will be sustained if the demand for imports stays constant. This can only be achieved at a higher real output with the same real exchange rate level; thus a rising real interest rate would shift the BB line to the right. Real output will rise at a given real exchange rate level, provided that producers employ a higher level of imported inputs at the same level of labor input, which would necessitate higher real wages through declining domestic prices.

The assumption that the Marshall-Lerner condition is satisfied is crucial to the conclusions of this model. In fact, this assumption ensures an upward sloping BB line in Figure 4.2. As is well known from the literature, substantial evidence supports the notion that the Marshall-Lerner condition may not be satisfied in the short run. The stability of the model requires the BB line to be steeper than the TT line, even if the Marshall-Lerner condition is not satisfied. As long as the BB line is steeper than the TT line and the current account deficit exogenous, none of the conclusions of this study are affected.

THE OUTCOME OF PAYMENTS CRISIS

Suppose that the economy is initially in a short-run equilibrium at a real exchange rate level, q_1, and a real output level, y_1, as in Figure 4.3. Any reduction in foreign borrowing shifts the BB line to the left and requires a real depreciation of the domestic currency and a decline in real output with constant domestic prices. In almost all cases where a payments crisis has been observed, governments have been reluctant to implement any kind of exchange rate policy, let alone a real depreciation. Assuming that the real exchange rate and the real interest rate remain

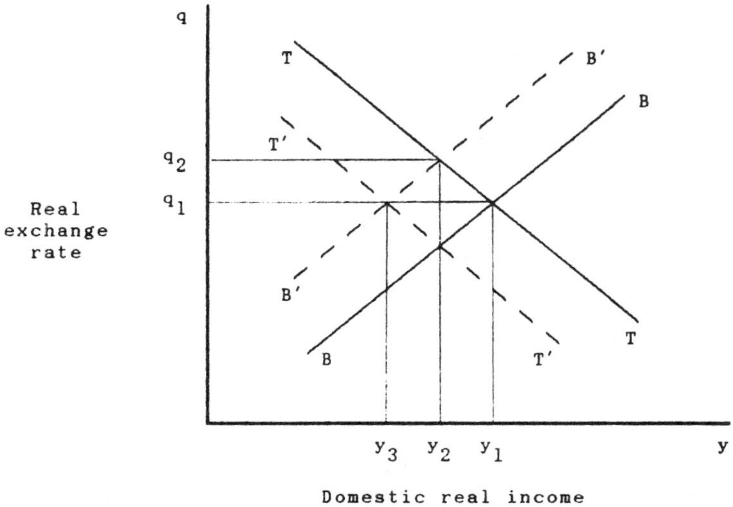

Figure 4.3. Effect of declining foreign borrowing on output.

constant, a lower current account deficit can only be achieved by decreases in imports, which could only result from declining real output. With sticky nominal wages and constant employment in the short run, however, this fall in real output would only be achieved by lower real wages causing the demand for imported inputs to decrease. Consequently, the decline in real wages in this scenario would result only from an increase in domestic prices.

In Figure 4.3, the new short-run equilibrium would be achieved by a shift in the TT line to the left, resulting in an equilibrium output at y_3. As previously noted, the model generates an inverse Phillips curve between prices and real output. The decline in real output along with rising prices, a common feature of economic performance in countries with payments crises, is by no means unavoidable but rather a result of the failure of countries to adopt the appropriate real exchange rate and real interest rate policies.

A decline in foreign borrowing could be accommodated by an increase in the real interest rate, which would decrease the demand for imports without much of an adverse output effect. In this case, the real exchange rate and real interest rate policies can be used in a complementary way to prevent output loss and price increases resulting from a lower level of foreign borrowing.[7]

From a purely macroeconomic viewpoint, international payments crises are the result of the failure of countries to implement appropriate real exchange rate (and real interest rate) policies. The experiences of those countries that have successfully faced payments crises or avoided their consequences in a short period of time, notably South Korea and Turkey, suggest that additional foreign borrowing is an option as long as the growth in exports is larger than the growth in total foreign debt. This casual observation alone seems to be sufficient to prove that one cannot overemphasize the role of real exchange rate policies in stabilization programs which ultimately need additional foreign borrowing.

AN EMPIRICAL ANALYSIS

The model discussed in the preceding sections is difficult to test empirically because data on nominal wages and total foreign borrowing are not readily available. The model states an important relationship between two policy variables (the real exchange rate and the real interest rate) and two target variables (real output and prices); that is, *an increase in the real interest rate or a depreciation of the domestic currency will increase real output and reduce inflation.*

The empirical analysis in this section concentrates on testing this proposition in a vector autoregression (VAR) framework as suggested in Sims (1980a, 1980b). In a four-equation unrestricted vector autoregression model, only the variables that we are interested in are included: the real interest rate, the rate of change in the real exchange rate, output growth, and the rate of inflation.[8]

Data

The data used in this study are compiled monthly. The percentage changes in the real exchange rate index, output, and prices are computed every twelve months to assure the stability of the system. The real exchange rate index is computed by the end-of-period nominal exchange rate of the Turkish lira vis-à-vis the weighted average of the U.S. dollar and the German mark, each with a weight of 50 percent. In computing the real exchange rate, industrial prices in the U.S. and Germany are used, while prices in Turkey are measured by the wholesale price index published by the Treasury of the Republic of Turkey.

Since a monthly real GNP, or industrial output index, is not yet available for the Turkish economy, an interpolation method is used to derive the monthly path of real GNP based on the year-end value of real GNP. In the interpolation process a statistical relation between yearly GNP and yearly production of selected industrial goods on which monthly data are available is exploited.[9]

The real interest rate is computed by taking the highest compounded yearly interest rate on time deposits deflated by the last twelve-month percentage change in the wholesale price index.

Empirical Results

In this four-equation VAR model, six lags of each variable are found to be sufficient to represent the system. Each equation is estimated using data from July 1975 to December 1985, and a constant term and a dummy variable distinguishing the post-January 1980 period from the previous period is employed. In this simple framework, three different, but by no means independent, approaches will be presented to quantify the response of output and prices to real interest rate and real exchange rate policies.

The first set of results concerning the block exogeneity of output growth and price changes with respect to the real interest rate and exchange policies are presented in Table 4.1. A Granger causality test is performed to test the hypothesis that the real interest rate and/or the real exchange rate has no effect on output changes and/or price changes. If the F-statistics probabilities are above the critical value, this hypothesis cannot be rejected. As seen from Table 4.1, at the 10 percent level of marginal significance one can reject the hypothesis that the real exchange rate and the real interest rate do not separately cause changes in the rates of output growth and prices. Although not reported, causality in the opposite direction cannot be found, except from domestic price changes to the real exchange rate. This finding lends some support to the notion that the authorities can

TABLE 4.1 Results Exogeneity Tests, F-Tests Probabilities

		Variables Caused	
	Rates	Output	Price
Variables Causing	Real Interest Rate	0.0915	0.0269
	Real Exchange Rate	0.0656	0.00001

influence the output growth and the rate of inflation in Turkey through real interest rate and real exchange rate policies.

The direction of output and price responses to these policies can be observed by plotting the standardized moving average coefficients of the system. Figure 4.4 shows the response of output growth and price changes to a positive one-unit shock of one standard deviation in the real interest rate, while Figure 4.5 shows the response of the same variables to a positive one-unit shock of one standard deviation in the real exchange rate. The positive shock in the real exchange rate is an appreciation of the Turkish lira. It is evident that standardized shocks in both the real exchange rate and the real interest rate have similar impacts on both the rate of output growth and inflation. In both cases, a real depreciation of the Turkish lira and an increase in the real interest rate will increase the rate of growth in real output while reducing the rate of inflation. These findings provide indirect support for the proposition developed in the previous sections.

The magnitude of the effects of real exchange rate and real interest rate policies on output growth and inflation is presented in Table 4.2. The unrestricted four-equation VAR model is used to decompose the forecast variance of each variable in terms of innovations in all other variables and in itself. Table

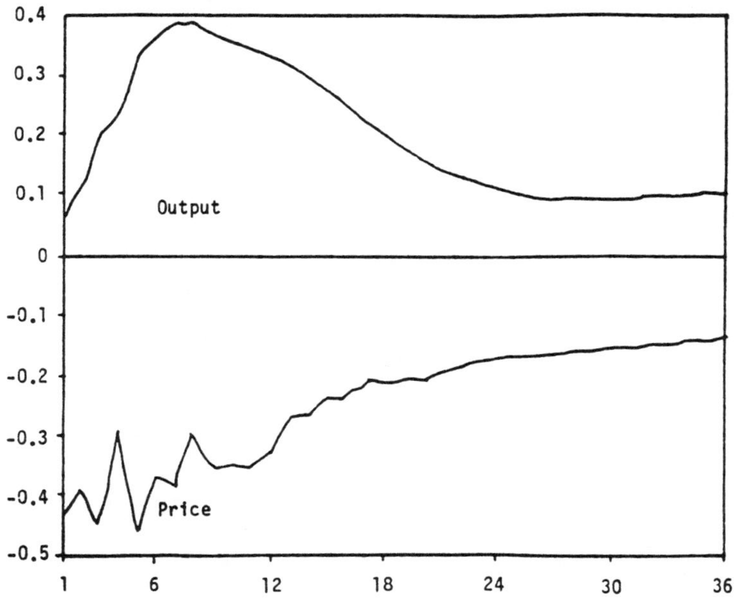

Figure 4.4. Innovations in real interest rate.

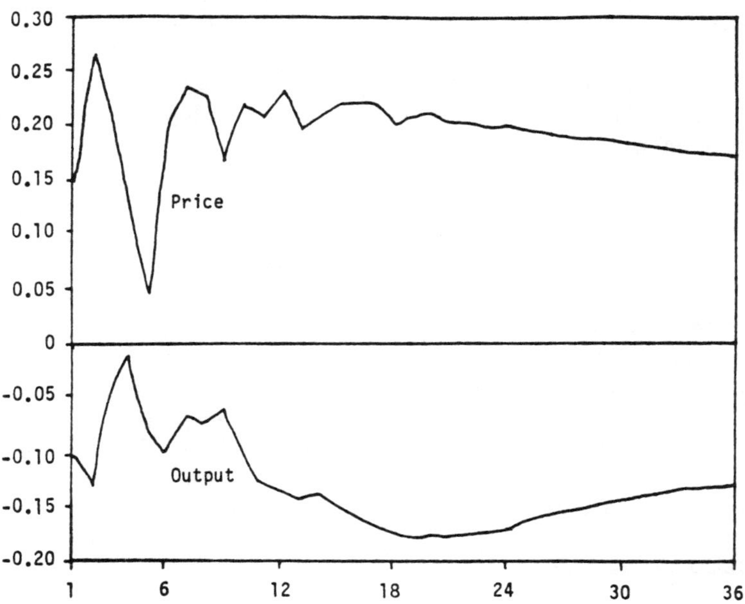

Figure 4.5. Innovations in real exchange rate.

TABLE 4.2 Variance Decompositions

Innovations in	Period	Output	Price
Real Interest Rate	1	1.25	35.78
	6	13.72	37.08
	12	23.78	37.84
	18	26.28	35.83
	24	25.72	34.19
Real Exchange Rate	1	3.68	3.81
	6	16.84	7.31
	12	21.18	10.66
	18	41.30	13.14
	24	64.55	15.24

4.2 presents only the decomposition of the forecast variance in output growth and inflation in terms of innovations in the real exchange rate and the real interest rate. As can be seen, innovations in the real interest rate explain more than 23 percent of the forecast variance in output growth and 37 percent of the forecast variance in inflation within the first twelve months. Similarly, innovations in the real exchange rate explain 21 percent of the forecast variance in output growth and 10 percent of the forecast variance in inflation within a year, 64 percent for output growth and 15 percent for inflation within 24 months. Although not reported, the feedback from output growth and inflation to the real exchange rate and the real interest rate is not very large, which suggests that the remaining forecast variance of output growth and inflation can be explained by innovations in these variables alone. The real exchange rate, however, is an important policy tool in manipulating real output growth, while the real interest rate can be effective in controlling inflation in the short run.

CONCLUDING REMARKS

The theoretical model under discussion fits the Turkish experience in the last decade well and explains an upward-sloping Phillips curve. In particular, it demonstrates the importance of real exchange rate and real interest rate policies in any stabilization program. Unsuccessful stabilization efforts result from a failure to implement liberal exchange rate and interest rate policies. In this regard, the Turkish experience constitutes a good example. As is well documented in Canevi (1984), no stabilization attempt will be successful if exchange rates are not part of, or not seriously considered a part of, stabilization policy packages.

Both theoretical exercises and empirical results suggest several lessons for policy makers. In order of importance, these would be the following:

1. Real depreciation of domestic currency is a necessary component of a successful economic program. It should be implemented without fearing inflation in the short run.
2. Reasonably high interest rates are an integral part of a successful economic program. Real interest rate policy should not be considered a substitute but rather a complement to a real exchange rate policy.
3. In the long run, control over inflation must occur through money supply policy; hence, ways to control the money supply must be explored while leaving interest rate determination to the market.

NOTES

The author is grateful to Patrick Conway, Patricia Lasonde, and Libby Rittenberg for their suggestions. The initial work was done when the author was visiting the Research Department of the Central Bank of the Republic of Turkey. The views expressed and any shortcomings are the responsibility of the author alone.

1. See Mundell (1968) and Fleming (1962).

2. The perfect substitution of imported consumption goods for imported intermediate goods does not affect the qualitative conclusions of this study, although it greatly simplifies the exposition.

3. Noting that the creditworthiness of a country is closely related to its level of exports and growth performance (Derviş and Petri 1987), one can easily assume that the foreign borrowing constraint is a

function of exports and real income. In this case, while conclusions of this exposition will not change in any qualitative way, the impact of policy variables on the price level and output will be stronger.

4. The Marshall-Lerner condition in this context is that the sum of absolute values of the export supply elasticity and the import demand elasticity is greater than one. For a full explanation of the Marshall-Lerner condition, see Chacholiades (1978).

5. While these assumptions seem to be overly restrictive, they can be justified in the case of the Turkish economy. Casual observation suggests that employment in Turkey is not as volatile as output, and nominal wage adjustment is not instantaneous. Common practice in the literature assumes fixed nominal wages and/or slow adjustment of labor in production in the short run. See, for example, Kumcu (1985), Brecher (1974), and Bhagwati and Johnson (1961).

6. In fact, the model provides a solution for real income and prices. However, for expositional purposes the author chose to present the model graphically in the real income-real exchange axes.

7. For similar conclusions, see Saracoglu (1985) and Canevi (1984).

8. As the contemporaneous variance-covariance matrix of innovations cannot be assumed to be diagonal, the order in which these variables are stacked in VAR will matter. The results presented come from the following ordering: real interest rate, real exchange rate, output growth rate, and the rate of inflation. Although several other orderings have been tried, the results do not vary substantially.

9. See *Monthly Statistical and Evaluation Bulletin*, (The Central Bank of the Republic of Turkey, June 1986).

REFERENCES

Bhagwati, J., and H. G. Johnson. 1961. The generalized theory of the effects of tariffs on the terms of trade. *Oxford Economic Papers* 13:225-53.

Brecher, R. A. 1974. Minimum wage rates and the pure theory of international trade. *Quarterly Journal of Economics* 88:98-116.

Brito, D. L., and J. D. Richardson. 1975. Some disequilibrium dynamics of exchange rate changes. *Journal of International Economics* 5:1-13.

Canevi, Y. 1984. Role of stabilization policies in the world debt problem: The Turkish experience. Speech delivered at the conference on LDC Financing--Managing the Way Back, 6-9 May, at the Federal Reserve Bank of New York, New York City.

Central Bank of the Republic of Turkey. 1986. *Monthly Statistical and Evaluation Bulletin*. Ankara, June.

Chacholiades, M. 1978. *International Trade Theory and Policy*. New York: McGraw-Hill.

Derviş, K., and P. Petri. 1987. The macroeconomics of successful development: What are the lessons? Paper presented for the NBER Conference on Macroeconomics, March 13-14, Cambridge, Mass.

Fleming, M. 1962. Domestic financial policies under fixed and floating exchange rates. *International Monetary Fund Staff Paper* 9:369-79.

Kumcu, M. E. 1985. The theory of commercial policy in a monetary economy with sticky wages. *Journal of International Economics* 18:159-70.

Mundell, R. A. 1968. *International Economics*. London: Macmillan.

Saracoglu, R. 1985. The role of real exchange rates in stabilization policies: The case of Turkey. Paper presented at a colloquium for the executive directors of the World Bank, November, Washington D.C.

Sims, C. A. 1980a. Macroeconomics and reality. *Econometrica* 48:1-48.

______. 1980b. Comparison of interwar and postwar business cycles: Monetarism reconsidered. *American Economic Review* 70:250-57.

5

Money Supply Responses to Exogenous Shocks in Turkey

MAXWELL J. FRY

The standard approach to modeling central bank behavior in developed countries starts with the central bank's objective function. Objectives typically include inflation, unemployment, and international reserve targets. The central bank has instruments such as the discount rate, discount quotas, and open-market operations to affect the cash base, and reserve requirements and credit ceilings to affect the money supply multiplier. It has a macroeconomic model that indicates how its instruments directly or indirectly affect the target variables. The final step is to construct and estimate reaction functions that relate movements in the instruments to changes in the targeted variables (Black 1983).

Direct application of this approach to Turkey is inappropriate for a number of reasons. Until very recently, the Central Bank of Turkey did not use any macroeconomic model for monetary policy purposes. Economic policy in general, and monetary policy in particular, was not based on the belief that the stock of money had any influence on either prices or output. Until 1980 institutional interest rates fixed by administrative decision were changed very infrequently and were certainly not used as an instrument of macroeconomic policy.

The Central Bank of Turkey seems to have followed the real bills doctrine with respect to domestic credit expansion to the private sector; it made credit available to meet needs of trade. Its first objective, therefore, might be regarded as maintaining some ratio of private-sector domestic credit to nominal GNP. A second objective has been to increase credit when the country's foreign exchange receipts rose so that a larger volume of capital equipment and raw materials imports could be financed. In other words, rather than contracting domestic credit to sterilize foreign exchange inflows, the Central Bank reacted by expanding domestic credit. The only other central bank objective seems to have been an attempt to reduce imports by imposing import predeposits when net foreign assets ran dangerously low.

A major constraint on the Central Bank's behavior has been the obligation to finance the government's borrowing requirements. Since virtually no attention has been paid to the money stock, an expansion in domestic credit to the government sector has not been countered by any significant squeeze of private sector credit.

Net foreign assets have been affected negatively by domestic credit expansion and positively by factors raising money demand, as anticipated by the monetary approach to the balance of payments. At various times, however, the Turkish Government tightened restrictions on foreign trade and payments in attempts to reduce the balance of payments deficit (Krueger 1974). These restrictions succeeded in stemming the loss of foreign exchange reserves in response to domestic credit expansion. They thus reduced the spillover of excess domestic demand caused by domestic credit expansion into imports.

This chapter extends my earlier work (1980b, 1986b) on inflation and growth in Turkey. The models presented in those papers treated the money supply as exogenous. Here I treat the money supply as endogenous and analyze Turkey's money supply process in an attempt to provide a more complete explanation of the inflationary accelerations in monetary growth that occurred in the 1950s and 1970s.

The rate of growth (logarithmic trend) in the money stock broadly defined averaged 8.1 percent annually over the period 1941-50. It accelerated to 19.0 percent, 1951-58; fell to 14.8 percent, 1959-70; and increased again to 36.4 percent, 1971-85. The two periods of more rapid monetary growth were accompanied by the two bouts of double digit inflation that have taken place in

Turkey since World War II. After a decade during which inflation averaged 2.2 percent, the continuously compounded trend rate of growth in the GNP deflator rose to 15.1 percent in the years 1954-59, declined to 5.4 percent, 1960-70; and accelerated to 32.8 percent 1971-85.

Turkey's recent inflation started its explosive stage during 1977-79. The annual inflation rate measured by the wholesale price index accelerated from 18 percent in the first quarter of 1977 to 119 percent in the first quarter of 1980. As measured by the continuously compounded rate of change in the GNP deflator (the index actually used in the model), inflation rose from 22 percent in 1977 to 71 percent in 1980 (see Table 5.1).

Concomitant with this price explosion was an equally alarming decline in the rate of economic growth. Real GNP grew by over 7 percent a year between 1974 and 1976. The growth rate fell to 2.8 percent (continuously compounded) in 1978 and was negative in both 1979 and 1980. Given the behavior of prices, the falling growth rate can hardly be attributed to deficient demand. Rather, as will be explained in detail, Turkish inflation caused a severe credit squeeze (as well as an acute balance of payments crisis). Output growth was constrained from the supply side in part by the lack of finance.

In 1981, Turkey's rate of economic growth rose to a continuously compounded rate of 4.1 percent. In this year the nominal twelve-month time deposit rate of interest was increased dramatically to 50 percent, raising the real deposit rate by 18 percentage points to its highest level in nine years. In 1982 monetary expansion slowed somewhat, and the real deposit rate became positive for the first time since 1970.

Turkey experienced a similar episode of accelerating inflation and declining growth between 1955 and 1960. The pattern of events in the 1970s seems to have followed inexorably the script of the 1950s. Both inflations appear to have been triggered by rapid increases in foreign exchange receipts (see Tables 5.1 and 5.2). The sharp increase in the 1950s was caused by the Korean War boom and a large increase in agricultural exports. The rise in the early 1970s was due to a very substantial increase in remittances from Turkish workers in Germany as well as the commodity boom.

TABLE 5.1 Money, Interest, Inflation, and Growth Rates, 1950-85[a]

Date	GNP Growth Rate	Inflation Rate	Money Growth Rate	Velocity of Circulation	Nominal Deposit Rate	Real Deposit Rate
1950	8.9	-2.1	5.8	5.8	6.5	5.9
1951	12.1	6.3	17.6	5.8	5.9	3.1
1952	11.3	2.7	17.7	5.6	5.0	2.0
1953	10.7	4.7	19.4	5.4	5.0	1.4
1954	-3.0	5.0	17.1	4.6	5.0	1.0
1955	7.6	10.7	16.2	4.7	5.0	-1.1
1956	3.1	11.2	23.4	4.3	5.0	-3.0
1957	7.5	20.9	24.4	4.5	5.0	-7.2
1958	4.4	13.3	14.8	4.6	5.0	-8.1
1959	4.0	18.1	10.8	5.2	5.0	-10.1
1960	3.4	3.3	11.8	4.9	5.0	-7.1
1961	2.0	4.0	8.9	4.8	5.8	-3.9
1962	6.0	9.1	9.3	5.1	6.5	-2.7
1963	9.2	5.6	10.9	5.3	6.5	-1.3
1964	4.0	2.5	13.5	4.9	6.5	0.6
1965	3.1	4.2	16.6	4.5	6.5	1.4
1966	11.3	6.2	20.2	4.3	6.5	1.2
1967	4.1	6.3	18.1	4.0	6.5	0.8
1968	6.5	3.8	15.0	3.8	6.5	1.3
1969	5.3	5.2	15.1	3.7	6.5	1.3
1970	5.6	11.2	17.2	3.7	7.3	0.2
1971	9.7	16.8	22.3	3.8	9.0	-1.4
1972	7.2	15.2	24.0	3.8	9.0	-3.3
1973	5.2	20.0	24.1	3.8	9.0	-6.1
1974	7.1	25.0	23.9	4.1	9.0	-9.7
1975	7.7	15.0	23.8	4.1	9.0	-9.4
1976	7.6	15.5	22.8	4.1	9.0	-9.0
1977	3.9	21.9	25.3	4.1	9.0	-10.3
1978	2.8	36.3	30.2	4.5	11.3	-13.5
1979	-0.4	53.7	40.1	5.1	17.3	-17.5
1980	-1.1	71.2	49.7	6.3	26.5	-22.3
1981	4.0	35.0	57.9	5.2	49.2	-4.4
1982	4.5	24.2	51.2	4.2	50.0	0.9
1983	3.3	24.6	32.5	4.0	42.7	0.1
1984	6.0	40.1	36.2	4.4	51.4	5.2
1985	4.9	36.1	45.5	4.2	53.0	7.0

Sources: Same as in Table 5.2.

[a] All rates except the nominal deposit rate of interest are continuously compounded. The method of estimating the average money stock in each year rests on two assumptions: Nominal GNP grows smoothly over the year, velocity of circulation is constant during the year. First the average daily growth rate in the money stock from the end of the previous year to the end of the current year is calculated. Then this growth rate is used as the daily interest rate to calculate the value of an ordinary annuity (sinking fund) after 365 daily payments equal to the end of last year's money stock. Each daily payment earns interest at the daily rate until the end of the year. Finally, the value of the annuity at the end of the year is divided by 365.

TABLE 5.2 Money, Domestic Credit, Net Foreign Assets, and Foreign Exchange Receipts as Percentage of Nominal GNP, 1950-85

Date	ΔM/YP[a]	ΔDC/YP[b]	ΔNFA/YP[c]	F/YP[d]
1950	2.3	6.5	-1.3	6.9
1951	3.7	4.8	-0.8	8.9
1952	2.6	6.9	-2.2	9.5
1953	4.5	10.1	1.0	10.6
1954	2.3	7.2	-1.1	7.7
1955	4.6	8.7	-0.9	6.4
1956	5.7	6.2	0.5	5.5
1957	5.4	8.2	-0.3	3.5
1958	1.3	3.9	0.3	3.9
1959	3.0	4.0	-0.2	4.8
1960	1.8	2.1	0.6	2.5
1961	2.0	-1.0	0.9	6.7
1962	1.8	4.2	-0.3	11.0
1963	2.4	4.8	-0.4	9.4
1964	3.4	3.0	0.4	8.2
1965	3.9	5.6	0.3	8.0
1966	4.8	6.4	-0.7	7.3
1967	3.6	4.2	0.0	6.1
1968	4.0	1.7	0.9	7.0
1969	4.1	6.3	1.0	6.9
1970	5.3	4.0	-1.5	3.6
1971	6.5	5.8	2.9	10.4
1972	6.2	6.1	0.6	10.2
1973	6.6	5.7	2.2	11.9
1974	5.6	8.9	-2.2	10.4
1975	6.1	13.1	-3.8	8.6
1976	5.2	12.7	-5.5	6.0
1977	7.1	13.8	-2.1	9.9
1978	6.9	10.8	-2.2	5.2
1979	9.4	14.9	-2.4	5.1
1980	8.1	16.6	-6.1	7.6
1981	12.3	12.1	0.3	14.2
1982	9.8	12.7	-0.9	12.3
1983	6.4	11.8	-3.5	11.8
1984	10.5	20.6	-6.7	10.8
1985	10.8	19.6	-8.0	10.7

Sources: State Institute of Statistics,(1984:33-34), Central Bank (1982:115, 126; 1984:8) and IMF, *International Financial Statistics*, computer tape; World Bank, *Bank Economic and Social Database*, computer tape.

[a]ΔM/YP - Change in money (December to December) as percentage of nominal GNP.
[b]ΔDC/YP - Change in domestic credit as percentage of nominal GNP.
[c]ΔNFA/YP - Change in net foreign assets as percentage of nominal GNP.
[d]F/YP - Foreign exchange receipts adjusted for exchange rate changes as percentage of nominal GNP.

Initially the larger foreign exchange receipts raised net foreign assets. Rather than sterilizing the effect of higher net foreign assets on the money supply, the Central Bank responded by expanding domestic credit to finance a greater volume of capital equipment and raw materials imports. Although this reduced rapidly the level of net foreign assets, it sustained the expansionary monetary impulse. The Central Bank then followed the real bills doctrine toward domestic credit expansion, accommodating demand pressures generated by the accelerating rise in nominal GNP.

Accelerated monetary growth produced inflation. This in turn enlarged the public-sector deficit due to the lag in the collection of tax receipts, erosion of the tax base, and price freezes on products of the state economic enterprises. The public-sector deficit was financed by further increases in the money supply, thus adding fuel to the inflationary fire.

A small-scale macroeconomic model of the Turkish economy in which money is endogenous along with inflation and the rate of economic growth is presented here. The model incorporates the deposit rate of interest as a determinant of both inflation and growth to explain the negative relationship between inflation and growth. A dynamic simulation of the model tracks rather successfully what actually happened to the rate of monetary growth over the period 1976-85.

THE MONEY SUPPLY PROCESS

This section offers an explanation of the money supply process in Turkey over the period 1951-85. This macroeconomic model contains six equations, four of them explaining components of the money supply. The money supply model analyzed here starts with the consolidated balance sheet of the central and commercial banks:

$$M2 = DCp + NDCg + NFA - NOI, \tag{5.1}$$

where M2 is money broadly defined to include time and savings deposits as well as currency in circulation and demand deposits, DCp is domestic credit to the private sector, NDCg is net domestic credit to the government or public sector, NFA is net foreign asset, and NOI is net other items. Changes in the money stock are taken here to be the residual outcome of overall changes on the right hand side of equation (5.1); hence movements in domestic credit, net foreign assets, and net other items explain in combination changes in the money supply.

The exogenous variables that do most of the work in this model are foreign exchange receipts, terms of trade, and the nominal deposit rate of interest (see Tables 5.1 and 5.2). An increase in foreign exchange receipts not only directly raises net foreign assets, but also stimulates domestic credit expansion to the private sector. A decline in the terms of trade also elicits domestic credit expansion to the private sector. A rise in the deposit rate of interest increases net foreign assets.

Turkey's disequilibrium interest-rate system ensures that there is always excess demand for institutional credit at the administratively fixed rates of interest. Until 1981 the government fixed ceilings for virtually all nominal institutional interest rates in Turkey. These ceilings were binding throughout the postwar period. The ceiling on the twelve-month time deposit rate typifies the inflexibility of the system. Between 1951 and 1961 the deposit rate was 5 percent compounded annually (see Table 5.1). It was raised to 6.5 percent in 1961, to 9 percent in 1970, and to 12 percent in 1978. Loan rate ceilings were also adjusted only in those years.

On the other hand, the inflation rate varied considerably over this period. Clearly, therefore, the real twelve-month deposit rate of interest, calculated as the continuously compounded nominal deposit rate minus the continuously compounded expected rate of inflation, fluctuated widely and changed roughly in the opposite direction to the inflation rate.

As explained in more detail elsewhere (Fry 1986b), the government took a first step toward introducing a more flexible interest rate policy in May 1979 when the twelve-month deposit rate was raised from 12 to 20 percent. The effect of this substantial increase in the nominal deposit rate on the real deposit rate was more than erased by an increase in the inflation rate from 36 percent in 1978 to 54 percent in 1979.

The government took a second step toward interest rate flexibility in 1980. As part of the stabilization program implemented under a standby agreement with the International Monetary Fund, the Turkish Government deregulated interest rates on time deposits in July

1980. The twelve-month time deposit rate rose immediately to 33 percent, a rate determined through cartel agreement by the large commercial banks (Kopits 1984:4). That a cartel would step in if the government stepped out of the business of setting institutional rates of interest was quite predictable (Fry 1980b:543). The July 1980 deposit rate increase was still insufficient to counteract the acceleration in inflation to 71 percent in that year; the real deposit rate of interest declined steadily until 1981.

Under some competitive pressure from increasingly attractive yields on government bonds, the bank cartel raised the twelve-month deposit rate in two steps to 50 percent by February 1981. Despite an acceleration in the continuously compounded rate of monetary growth from 50 percent in 1980 to 58 percent in 1981, the inflation rate was halved from 71 to 35 percent. At the same time the rate of economic growth increased from -1.1 percent in 1980 to 4.0 percent in 1981.

As I argue elsewhere (1986b), both the reduction in inflation and the acceleration in economic growth can be attributed to the 18-percentage-point increase in the real deposit rate of interest between 1980 and 1981. The consequent increase in money demand, illustrated by the rapid reduction in velocity of circulation from 6.3 to 5.2 between 1980 and 1981, reduced inflation and at the same time relieved the credit squeeze that had previously been stifling economic growth. A 4-percentage-point increase in the real deposit rate in 1982 was accompanied by a further reduction in the inflation rate to 24 percent. The rate of economic growth rose to 4.5 percent while velocity of circulation declined to 4.2, a figure comparable to velocities found in the more stable years of the late 1960s and early 1970s (see Table 5.1).

Interest-rate deregulation lasted only until January 1983 when the government again modified the interest-rate setting system. The nine largest banks were then bound by the interest-rate structure negotiated between the government and the bank cartel, while the other banks were allowed to offer a premium of 2.5 percentage points above these rates (Kopits 1984:4-5). With the decline in inflation, the nominal twelve-month time deposit rate was reduced to 45 percent in January 1983 and to 40 percent in July of the same year. As a result, the real deposit rate fell somewhat in 1983, and inflation hardly changed despite a decline in monetary growth from 51 percent in 1982 to 33 percent in 1983.

Foreign exchange receipts rose rapidly during 1981-83 (see Table 5.2). Monetary growth and inflation accelerated once again in 1984 and 1985. In fact, inflation had started to accelerate in the second half of 1983. Since the bank cartel was unwilling to raise nominal deposit rates, in December 1983 the government adopted yet another interest-rate setting system. Under it the Central Bank was authorized to review and set deposit rates at least every three months, taking into account fluctuations in the rate of inflation and other relevant economic developments. Under the new system the twelve-month deposit rate was increased again to 45 percent in mid-December 1983, and a three-month call deposit yielding 49 percent was reinstated.

The withholding tax on interest income was reduced (from 20 percent to 10 percent) at the end of 1983, as was the financial transactions tax on nonpreferential loan rates of interest (from 15 to 3 percent) (Kopits 1984:5). These two tax reforms together with the decline in the inflation rate substantially reduced the wedge between effective deposit and loan rates that had previously deterred financial intermediation (Fry 1979; Fry and Farhi 1979:366-73).

In conjunction with rationalization of reserve requirements and the introduction of deposit insurance in early 1983, the government appeared to have embarked upon a new course of financial development by the end of 1983. Despite an acceleration in monetary growth and inflation (40 percent in 1984 and 36 percent in 1985), real deposit rates rose in 1984 and 1985 to their highest levels since 1950. Velocity remained stable at its 1982 level of 4.2, down from 6.3 in 1980. Because of the high real deposit rates of interest, this latest inflationary surge was not accompanied by a credit squeeze in real terms. The rate of economic growth actually rose in 1984 to 6 percent, the highest rate of growth since 1976. Real GNP grew by 4.9 percent in 1985.

This interest-rate setting system implies that the nominal quantity of institutional credit has been determined solely by supply. Through rediscount and interest-rate ceilings, required reserve and liquidity ratios, the selective credit policy, and various informal pressures such as "persuading" the commercial banks to take up unsold government bonds, the monetary authorities have had strong influence over the volume and distribution of domestic credit. Furthermore, over 50 percent of commercial bank assets are held by state-owned special law banks. These assets are under the same degree of government control as the assets of the Central Bank. Domestic credit expansion is taken here to be determined by the monetary authorities--essentially the government, since the Central Bank has had virtually no autonomy since its establishment in 1930 (Fry 1972).

The econometric analysis covers the years 1951-85. This period appears to encompass at least two regimes. The first is associated with planned economic development during 1960-67 and the post-1980 years during which some restraining influence was exerted by the International Monetary Fund. The years 1960-67 and 1980-85 are hereafter called the stable years. The second consists of the unstable years of the Menderes government, 1950-59, and the period 1968-79, which started with student riots, followed by a series of increasingly weak civilian governments and ended with the military takeover of September 1980. The two regimes are distinguished in the econometric analysis by allowing coefficients of all variables to vary between one regime and the other.

Over the period 1951-85 the monetary authorities pursued a version of the real bills doctrine to a greater or lesser extent, sanctioning private sector credit expansion as they thought needs of trade dictated. Needs of trade as perceived by the monetary authorities are proxied by nominal GNP, YP. The monetary authorities also facilitated domestic credit expansion for the private sector to finance a higher level of capital equipment and raw materials imports when foreign exchange receipts, F, rose. The variable F is adjusted for exchange-rate changes and is treated as exogenous for reasons given by Hemphill (1974) and Krueger (1974:48-50). An insignificant reduction in domestic credit to the private sector was initiated to offset partially an increase in net domestic credit to the public sector, NDCg. A deterioration in the terms of trade, TT, seemed to elicit expansionary monetary policy either to finance inventory accumulation of export goods until their prices rose again or to finance higher import costs. With partial adjustment toward the desired level of private sector domestic credit, the lagged dependent variable becomes an additional explanatory variable.

A slope dummy (STAB) for the relatively stable years 1960-67 and 1980-85 was included initially for all the explanatory variables; however, only the slope dummy for the needs-of-trade variable, YP, was significant. The two-stage least-squares (2SLS) estimate of the supply function of domestic credit to the private sector in logarithmic form over the period 1951-85 is:

$$\begin{aligned} \ln(DCp) = {} & \underset{(-0.645)}{-\,0.328} + \underset{(1.728)}{0.302} \ln(\hat{YP}) - \underset{(-2.394)}{0.007} \ln(\hat{YP})\cdot STAB \\ & + \underset{(1.637)}{0.079} \ln(F) - \underset{(-0.336)}{0.040} \ln(NDCg) - \underset{(-3.518)}{0.283} \ln(TT) \\ & + \underset{(6.787)}{0.667} \ln(DCp)_{t-1}. \end{aligned} \tag{5.2}$$

$$\bar{R}^2 = 0.998 \quad DW = 1.84.$$

Domestic credit expansion in response to rising nominal GNP was reduced marginally during the years of the stable regime. In both regimes, however, domestic credit was expanded when foreign exchange receipts rose and the terms of trade deteriorated. Credit to the private sector was reduced (but insignificantly) when net domestic credit to the public sector rose.

Several models of self-generating inflation suggest that government deficits are due to lags in revenue collection (Aghevli and Khan 1977, 1978; Dutton 1971; Ness 1972; Uluatam 1973). In addition to lags in revenue collection, the tax base in Turkey was eroded by inflation, and prices of products of state economic enterprises were frozen as part of an anti-inflation strategy. The government's agricultural price support and procurement programs operated at increasing losses as domestic prices rose further above world prices at the increasingly overvalued exchange rate. Since government accounts are available only from 1968, net domestic credit to the government is used as a proxy for the government deficit. The 2SLS estimate of net domestic credit to the government, also in logarithmic form, for the 1951-85 period follows:

$$\ln(NDCg) = \underset{(4.214)}{5.133} + \underset{(4.489)}{0.967} \ln(\hat{P}) - \underset{(-3.690)}{0.192} \ln(\hat{P}) \cdot STAB$$

$$+ \underset{(3.462)}{0.461} \ln(NDCg)_{t-1}. \qquad (5.3)$$

$$\bar{R}^2 = 0.997 \quad DW = 1.82.$$

The self-generating inflation mechanism was dampened to a small but significant extent during the stable regime.

The monetary approach to the balance of payments indicates that net foreign assets are affected negatively by an increase in domestic credit (DC) and positively by factors that increase the demand for money (International Monetary Fund 1977; Johnson 1972). Exchange controls of greater severity during the periods 1953-58, 1964-70, and 1976-83 (Krueger 1974) dampened the impact of domestic credit expansion on the loss of foreign assets, as indicated by an additional slope dummy, RES, for these years. Given quantitative restrictions on imports and prohibition of capital outflows, net foreign assets increase when foreign exchange receipts rise. Lagged nominal GNP and the real deposit rate of interest, $d-\pi^e$, are used here as the determinants of nominal money demand. Since net foreign assets were negative over a substantial part of the observation period, the estimate is conducted in first-difference form with all variables except $d-\pi^e$ scaled by lagged nominal GNP to correct for heteroscedasticity:

$$\Delta NFA = - \underset{(-2.184)}{0.157} \Delta(\hat{DC}) - \underset{(-3.236)}{0.161} \Delta(\hat{DC}) \cdot STAB +$$

$$+ \underset{(1.684)}{0.076} \Delta(\hat{DC}) \cdot RES + \underset{(3.863)}{0.413} \Delta(F) + \underset{(0.435)}{0.011} \Delta(YP)_{t-1}$$

$$+ \underset{(2.441)}{0.286\Delta(d-\pi^e)} + \underset{(3.537)}{0.480\Delta(NFA)_{t-1}}. \qquad (5.4)$$

$$\bar{R}^2 = 0.816 \quad DW = 1.80.$$

An increase in domestic credit reduces net foreign assets, as expected. The negative effect of domestic credit expansion on net foreign assets is greater during the periods of economic stability (STAB) but is dampened during the three periods of tighter foreign trade and payments restrictions (RES). Even in unrestrictive stable years, the offset coefficient of -0.32 is only about half the magnitude of offset coefficients estimated for OECD countries (Laskar 1983:329). The increase in net foreign assets produced by a rise in foreign exchange receipts, however, is the key to understanding the start of both inflationary episodes in postwar Turkey. A rise in the previous year's GNP and the following year's real deposit rate increase net foreign assets, as anticipated by the monetary approach to the balance of payments.

Import predeposits constitute an important component of net other items. The requirement to deposit some Turkish liras in advance of importation has been varied with respect to both percentage and duration. The authorities raised import predeposits gradually when net foreign assets declined. The OLS estimate of the change in net other items is

$$\Delta NOI = \underset{(3.693)}{0.019} - \underset{(-2.760)}{0.514\Delta(NFA)_{t-1}} + \underset{(2.371)}{0.518\Delta(NFA)_{t-1}\cdot STAB}$$

$$+ \underset{(0.101)}{0.018\Delta(NOI)_{t-1}}. \qquad (5.5)$$

$$\bar{R}^2 = 0.124 \quad DW = 2.04.$$

Falling net foreign assets were accompanied by rising net other items (import predeposits) except during the stable periods. During these years declining net foreign assets decreased net other items, probably due to the revaluation of foreign exchange after devaluations. An increase in net foreign assets due to devaluation raises net worth, another component of NOI.

Equations (5.2) through (5.5) purport to explain the behavior of the money supply in Turkey during the period 1951-85. Dynamic simulations of this money supply model reported in the fourth section suggest that the stability of this money supply process is fragile. The rapid rise in foreign exchange receipts in the early 1970s causes an explosive acceleration in the simulated monetary growth rate. Once inflation gets under way, the feedback mechanism from inflation to monetary acceleration through the widening public sector deficit can also produce explosive monetary acceleration unless foreign exchange receipts fall sufficiently rapidly under a fixed and increasingly overvalued exchange rate.

Whether or not Turkey's money supply system is unstable, both postwar inflations were certainly accompanied by increasing political instability. The 1950s' inflation was brought to a halt after a massive devaluation, rescheduling of international debts, introduction of an austerity/stabilization program, and the military coup of 1960. The 1970s' inflation was contained only after several devaluations, a series of debt reschedulings, the introduction of a stabilization program in conjunction with a standby agreement with the International Monetary Fund, and a military takeover of government in 1980.

Substantial increases in foreign exchange receipts seem to have set the inflationary process in motion twice during the postwar period. Between 1950 and 1953 foreign exchange receipts increased from TL 670 million to TL 1650 million, that is, by 35 percent a year. They were still below their 1953 level in 1959, the year before devaluation. Foreign exchange receipts fluctuated between TL 5 billion and TL 6 billion between 1960 and 1966. From a level of TL 5.41 billion in 1962, they rose to TL 8.10 billion by 1969, that is, by under 6 percent a year. From 1972 to 1976 foreign exchange receipts rose from TL 32.03 billion to TL 84.88 billion, that is, by 27.5 percent a year.

INFLATION AND GROWTH

Inflation in Turkey is explained by the simple monetary model presented in Fry (1980b) and recently reestimated in Fry (1986b). Inflation is given as the difference between the rates of growth in per capita nominal money supply and per capita real money demand:

$$\pi = (\mu - \nu) - \Delta \ln(m^d), \quad (5.6)$$

where π is the inflation rate, μ is the rate of growth in the nominal money supply, ν is the population growth rate, and m^d is real per capita money demand.

Equation (5.6) is derived from the equilibrium condition in the money market: Demand equals supply. The credit market on the other hand remains in a disequilibrium condition whenever there is financial repression. Walras's law states that disequilibrium in one market must be matched by an equal and opposite disequilibrium in one or more other markets. It is natural to think of an excess demand for credit matched by an excess supply of money.

In fact, however, credit market disequilibrium can be viewed as an excess supply of bonds at the administratively fixed interest rate. This is matched by planned investment exceeding planned saving at that interest rate. In this case, planned investment does not represent effective investment demand since it is contingent upon obtaining investible funds at the fixed interest rate. Effective investment demand is curtailed by the lack of credit to equal saving forthcoming at the fixed interest rate. Demand for and supply of money can be equilibrated through price changes; hence money market equilibrium can coexist with disequilibrium in the credit market.

Prices tend to adjust relatively rapidly in many developing economies including Turkey because of the preponderance of auction markets and/or fast expectations responses (Lucas 1973). It may be reasonable to expect equilibrium in the money market to hold, at least for models intended for estimation using annual observations.

Real money demand is determined by one or more price variables and a budget constraint. Here the price variable chosen is the real deposit rate of interest $d-\pi^e$, where d is the nominal twelve-month time deposit rate of interest continuously compounded and π^e is expected inflation. Expected inflation is estimated using a second-order far-end constrained polynomial distributed lag in a per capita real money demand function estimated for the period 1950-85. This implies that tangible assets used as inflation hedges rather than bonds are the dominant substitute asset for broad money. Holdings of nonmonetary financial assets by the nonbank sector were in fact very limited in Turkey throughout the regression period. The budget constraint is per capita real permanent GNP, y^e. In contrast with the standard way of estimating permanent income, I estimate expected income growth and adjust last year's actual income level for expected income growth this year. This procedure can be justified by the fact that the rate of growth in GNP follows a random walk.

The 2SLS estimate of the inflation equation in Turkey for the period 1951-85 is

$$\pi = \underset{(18.413)}{1.096}(\hat{\mu}-\nu) - \underset{(-5.096)}{2.045}\Delta\ln(y^e) - \underset{(-5.386)}{1.641}\Delta(d-\pi^e), \quad (5.7)$$

$$\bar{R}^2 = 0.826 \quad DW = 1.65$$

where $\Delta\ln(y^e)$ is expected growth in per capita real GNP estimated as a second-order far-end constrained polynomial distributed lag. This estimate differs hardly at all from one covering 1950-77 reported in Fry (1980b:537), or from another for 1951-83 in Fry (1986b:103).

The coefficients of the three variables in equation (5.7) all agree with a priori expectations. The coefficient of the rate of change in the nominal money supply is not significantly different from one. The elasticity of money demand with respect to per capita real permanent income is about 2, a figure comparable with elasticities estimated directly in money demand studies using a broad definition of money. The coefficient of the change in the expected real deposit rate of interest of -1.64 is also of the same order of magnitude as coefficients estimated for Turkey and other developing countries in money demand functions (Abe et al. 1975; Fry 1978c; Fry and Farhi 1979: Ch. 4).

The short-run growth equation estimated here is a Fisherian Phillips curve with a credit availability effect added. The first determinant of the growth rate γ is the ratio of the actual to the expected price level P/P^e. This variable comes from extensions of the expectations-augmented Phillips curve in the late 1970s (Fry 1978a, 1978b; Korteweg 1978; Laidler 1978). If actual price exceeds expected price, entrepreneurs interpret the difference to reflect a real increase in demand for their products. Their response is to raise the rate of capacity utilization of the existing capital stock to increase output immediately and to invest more to increase that capacity. The higher P/P^e, the better the investment outlook appears and the greater the growth rate. Expected price P^e equals $\exp(\pi^e).P_{t-1}$. The expected inflation rate π^e used here is the same as that used in the inflation equation.

Expected inflation also affects short-term growth through the expected real deposit rate of interest $d-\pi^e$. Under Turkey's disequilibrium interest rate and exchange control systems, real money demand determines to a large extent the real supply of domestic credit because domestic credit is the primary asset backing the monetary liabilities of the banking system.

The traditional link between credit and output is through demand--the increase in credit created by monetary expansion is accompanied by an increase in demand which stimulates real output. Since 1973, however, a number of economists have focused on the link between credit and real output through the supply side (Buffie 1984; Fry 1980a; Kapur 1976; Keller 1980; Mathieson 1980; Taylor 1983; van Wijnbergen 1982, 1983). This Wicksellian view holds that the availability of working capital determines, ceteris paribus, the volume of production that can be financed. In particular, as Keller argues, ". . . production *expansion* may depend, entirely or in part, on credit availability and/or the cost of credit" (1980:455). Evidently this supply link between credit availability and real economic growth springs from the ratio of credit to output, or from the real rather than the nominal volume of credit.

Faster expansion of money and nominal credit raises the inflation rate. If the nominal deposit rate is fixed, the ensuing increase in expected inflation reduces the real deposit rate of interest--and this in turn reduces real money demand or decreases the ratio of money to nominal GNP. The ratio of domestic credit to nominal GNP, DC/Y, also falls even if domestic credit expansion is the cause of monetary acceleration. This is due to the fact that domestic credit expansion reduces net foreign assets by only a fraction of the credit expansion, as shown in equation (5.4). Thus, an acceleration in nominal domestic credit and hence in the money supply reduces credit availability in real terms.

As inflation accelerates and as real deposit rates,

real money demand, and real credit supply all decline, the government finds that the gap between conventional tax receipts and public expenditure widens. This gap is financed by heavier reliance on seigniorage and the inflation tax. The government extracts greater seigniorage by increasing the proportion of domestic credit allocated to the public sector and thus reduces the ratio of private sector credit to total domestic credit (DCp/DC). It levies an inflation tax by creating more money than the public wishes to hold at the current price level. This produces a double squeeze on credit available for private sector working capital. In other words, DCp/Y falls due to the decline in both DC/Y and DCp/DC when inflation accelerates in countries implementing selective credit policies through rigidly fixed nominal interest rate systems (Fry 1979, 1981, 1982a, 1982b; Kapur 1976; Mathieson 1979). In Turkey, for example, velocity of circulation rose by 70 percent and the ratio of public sector domestic credit to the money supply increased from 20 to 229 percent as the expected real deposit rate of interest fell from 0.2 percent in 1970 to -22.3 percent in 1980.

Turkey's private sector was starved of credit as the real supply of domestic credit declined and the government extracted a higher seigniorage from the money supply. Funds to finance working capital dried up, and the credit squeeze reduced the rate of capacity utilization of the existing fixed capital stock (Fry 1979); hence, the growth rate declined. In a reduced-form equation, $d-\pi^e$ has a positive effect on γ. This variable determines credit availability and also allocative efficiency of loanable funds.

In the longer run γ is determined by, among other factors, the volume and productivity of investment, both of which are affected positively by $d-\pi^e$ in Turkey (Fry 1979) and in several Asian developing countries (Fry 1980a, 1981, 1984, 1986a). In this model I assume that investment raises productive capacity--so moving the transformation frontier outward--smoothly over time. For industrial countries the time trend of real GNP may provide a reasonable proxy for normal supply--the noncyclical component of supply determined solely by productive capacity. For most developing countries, however, it is also necessary to take into account fluctuations in agricultural output. Year-to-year changes in the level of agricultural output are determined largely by variations in weather conditions; therefore, they represent exogenous shifts in the production possibility curve.

Trend growth in real GNP in Turkey differed significantly before and after the period 1962-76 (Fry 1971:322); therefore logarithmic trends in real GNP and agricultural output were calculated separately for 1948-61, 1962-76, and 1977-85. Normal supply is defined as trend real GNP plus the difference between the actual and trend real agricultural output.

Normal growth, γ^n, exerts a positive effect on γ. Above average growth in agricultural output and/or imports will depress growth in other sectors of the economy as a result of an additional credit effect. Credit requirements of Turkey's agricultural price support program, which are of course positively related to growth in agricultural output, have had priority over credit demands of other sectors. Hence the other sectors suffer a credit squeeze in real terms when more of the fixed real supply of domestic credit is allocated to agriculture and imports. All this implies that the effect of γ^n on γ is positive but that the coefficient of γ^n will be somewhat less than one. Above average growth in agricultural output and/or imports imposes a credit squeeze on the other sectors, reduces their rates of capacity utilization, and so produces below average growth there.

The 2SLS estimate of the growth equation in Turkey for the period 1951-85 is as follows:

$$\gamma = \underset{(8.585)}{0.957(\gamma^n)} + \underset{(1.304)}{0.009(\hat{P}/P^e)} + \underset{(3.039)}{0.154(d-\pi^e)}. \quad (5.8)$$

$$\bar{R}^2 = 0.731 \quad DW = 1.95.$$

Equation (5.7) shows that an acceleration in nominal monetary growth raises the inflation rate and thus P/P^e. In turn an increase in P/P^e raises growth in real GNP as shown in equation (5.8). This is the standard short-run Phillips curve tradeoff. When expected inflation rises so reducing P/P^e and $d-\pi^e$, the growth rate declines. In long-run equilibrium P equals P^e because inflation is fully anticipated. Then only the negative impact of a lower real deposit rate, $d-\pi^e$, is felt. With d held constant and below its market equilibrium level, the long-run Phillips curve produces a negative relationship between inflation and growth in a financially repressed economy like Turkey through the real credit supply mechanism, even before the effect of inflation on the saving rate and on the average efficiency of new investment is taken into account.

SIMULATIONS

Dynamic simulation of the six-equation money supply model developed and estimated in the second and the third sections requires the specification of forty-five identities. Equation (5.1) is used to calculate the simulated monetary stock. Expected inflation and income growth are calculated from the simulated inflation and real GNP growth rates. Simulated inflation and growth are combined to estimate nominal GNP growth and hence nominal GNP. Indeed, the nominal deposit rate of interest, normal growth, population growth, imports, the terms of trade, and the exchange rate are the only exogenous variables for simulation purposes.

Dynamic simulation of the six-equation model (equations 5.2, 5.3, 5.4, 5.5, 5.7, and 5.8) for the entire period 1951-85 produces a dramatic deflation in the second half of the 1950s (inflation of -25 percent in both 1957 and 1958) due to the substantial decline in foreign exchange receipts during that time. By 1975, however, monetary growth explodes because of the large increase in foreign exchange receipts in the early 1970s. Starting the dynamic simulation in 1974 delayed the explosive monetary growth until 1978.

The last decade survives without a simulated monetary explosion when the dynamic simulation starts in 1976. Indeed the model then tracks rather well what actually happened to the rate of growth in the money supply. The actual and simulated monetary growth rates are shown in Figure 5.1. It is apparent that the model succeeds in predicting the peak monetary growth rate in 1981 and the subsequent trough in 1983, albeit at rates somewhat lower than the actual ones. The correlation between actual and simulated monetary growth rates between 1976 and 1985 is 0.84.

This dynamic simulation underpredicts the changes in all four components of the monetary survey. By 1985

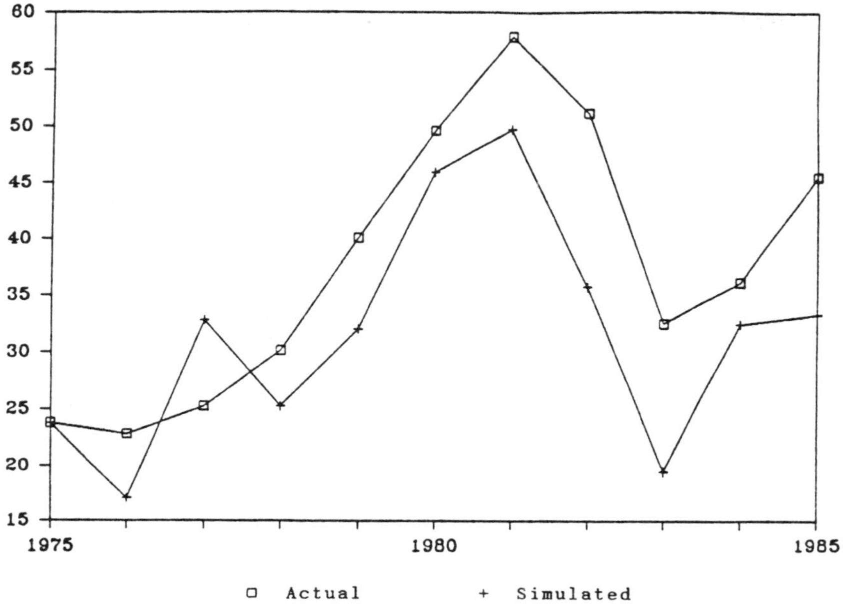

Figure 5.1. Actual and simulated rates of growth in the money stock, 1975-85. (Continously compounded percentage rates of change.)

net domestic credit to the government is underpredicted by the largest margin. On the other hand, net foreign assets are overpredicted.

Evidently the reductions in foreign exchange receipts in 1982 and 1983 (see Table 5.2), coupled with the rapid declines in inflation in 1981 and 1982, were sufficient to halt the acceleration in monetary growth. Both the actual and the simulated monetary growth rates fall in 1982 and 1983. Then, however, foreign exchange receipts stabilize and inflation accelerates, increasing the rates of domestic credit expansion and money growth.

The simulated inflation rate successfully predicts the peak 1980 inflation rate, as well as the subsequent rapid reduction in 1981. The simulated decline in

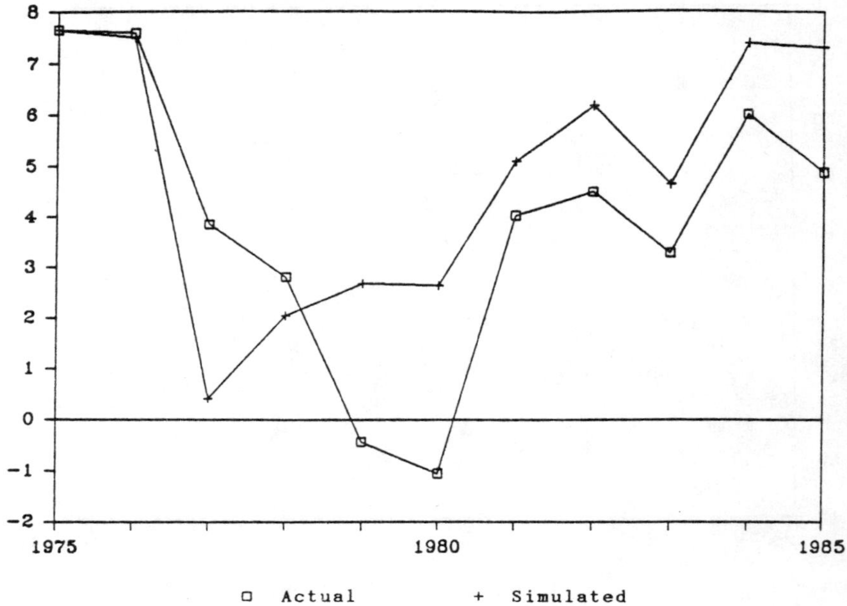

Figure 5.2. Actual and simulated rates of growth in real GNP, 1975-85. (Continuously compounded percentage rates of change.)

inflation in 1981, despite an 8-percentage-point increase in the monetary growth rate, comes from the large increase in the nominal deposit rate of interest that year. Inflation was decreased by a rapid increase in real money demand.

The model simulates the depression of 1977-80 fairly well on average but gets the timing wrong. Simulated and actual growth rates are shown in Figure 5.2. It predicts the 1981 recovery and subsequent improved growth rates quite successfully. In particular, the model predicts improved growth rates in 1984 and 1985 from the substantial increase in the real deposit rate of interest. The correlation between actual and simulated growth from 1976 to 1985 is 0.68.

The monetary authorities had at their disposal two

independent instruments of monetary policy to confront the inflationary surge of the late 1970s--the rate of growth in the nominal money supply and the nominal deposit rate of interest. There is in practice an upper bound to the deposit rate at its competitive market equilibrium rate (Fry 1980b:542). Here I assume that the nominal deposit rate lies below this upper bound.

The inflation and growth equations estimated in the third section show that a higher deposit rate of interest reduces inflation and raises the growth rate at the same time; therefore, an optimal monetary policy must set the nominal deposit rate at its upper bound. An obvious answer would be to abolish all institutional interest rate ceilings. In practice, however, the optimal competitive deposit rate has to be forced upon Turkey's cartelized and oligopolistic banking system (Fry 1972:Chs. 3, 4, 6) by fixing a *minimum* deposit rate and requiring banks to satisfy all deposit demand at this rate. This would be sufficient to produce the competitive result, provided loan demand were elastic at rates above the competitive loan rate of interest. The Turkish Government recognized the efficacy of financial liberalization in the 1980s. The effects have been impressive.

A dynamic simulation treating money as exogenous shows the effects of the interest-rate increases that occurred between 1979 and 1981 on inflation and growth. Table 5.3 also illustrates what might have happened had the twelve-month deposit rate of interest been held at 9 percent, its rate between 1970 and early 1978. Inflation would have been much higher than it actually was between 1978 and 1982. The simulation forecasts an inflation peak in 1981 at 99 percent and inflation rates of over 50 percent for four years in succession, 1979 through 1982.

This counterfactual dynamic simulation using a constant nominal deposit rate of interest also predicts much lower growth and declining real GNP for the seven years 1979-85. This simulation implies that the substantial increases in deposit rates were mainly responsible for Turkey's relatively small recession and reasonably rapid recovery after the stabilization program was initiated in 1980. It also shows just how much effect changes in the deposit rate can exert on both inflation and short-term growth.

TABLE 5.3 Dynamic Simulations with Exogenous Money Stock, 1975-85
(Continuously Compounded Percentage Rates of change)

ACTUAL

Date	Monetary Growth	Inflation Rate	Real GNP Growth	Real Deposit Rate
1975	23.8	15.0	7.7	-9.4
1976	22.8	15.5	7.6	-9.0
1977	25.3	21.9	3.9	-10.3
1978	30.2	36.3	2.8	-13.5
1979	40.1	53.7	-0.4	-17.5
1980	49.7	71.2	-1.1	-22.3
1981	57.9	35.0	4.0	-4.4
1982	51.2	24.2	4.5	0.9
1983	32.5	24.6	3.3	0.1
1984	36.2	40.1	6.0	5.2
1985	45.5	36.1	4.9	7.0

	BENCHMARK DYNAMIC SIMULATION			COUNTERFACTUAL SIMULATION WITH CONSTANT DEPOSIT RATE		
Date	Inflation Rate	Real GNP Growth	Real Deposit Rate	Inflation Rate	Real GNP Growth	Real Deposit Rate
1975	15.0	7.7	-9.4	15.0	7.7	-9.4
1976	-4.1	7.5	-3.2	9.4	7.0	-7.2
1977	45.8	0.4	-12.8	27.0	0.6	-10.4
1978	21.3	2.1	-11.1	41.3	1.3	-17.1
1979	26.0	2.7	-7.4	64.4	-0.4	-29.3
1980	47.2	2.6	-7.3	83.7	-2.9	-44.4
1981	16.0	5.1	12.7	99.4	-5.7	-60.6
1982	33.9	6.2	10.8	77.1	-5.6	-66.1
1983	14.6	4.6	10.0	32.1	-5.6	-55.9
1984	3.5	7.4	23.0	39.5	-3.7	-48.7
1985	24.5	7.3	23.1	60.0	-3.7	-48.5

CONCLUSION

The model of the money supply process in Turkey presented here is embedded in a small-scale macroeconomic model. The dynamic simulations support the basic premises of the money supply model. In particular, the estimated model predicts successfully the monetary accelerations following the three postwar episodes of substantial increases in foreign exchange receipts.

Accelerated monetary growth had a debilitating effect on the rate of economic growth in Turkey, at least until 1983. Over the period 1951-85 the correlation between monetary growth and inflation was 0.81. Even the short-run Phillips curve exhibits a negative relationship between inflation and economic growth. Over the period 1951-83 the correlation between inflation and growth is -0.45, while the correlation between monetary growth and economic growth is -0.29.

This small-scale macroeconomic model explains the negative correlation between inflation or monetary growth and economic growth through the effects of the real deposit rate of interest. Over the period 1951-83 the correlation between real deposit rate of interest and the rate of economic growth was 0.45. Over the same period the correlation between inflation and the real deposit rate of interest was -0.81, while between monetary growth and the real deposit rate it was -0.40. The real deposit rate moved inversely to the inflation rate because nominal rates of interest were adjusted so infrequently. When adjustments started to be made more frequently after 1983, the negative association disappeared, as did the negative association between inflation or monetary growth and the rate of economic growth. The counterfactual simulation for the 1976-85 period also illustrates the efficacy of monetary policy that makes active use of the deposit rate of interest under Turkey's disequilibrium interest rate system.

The importance attached by the model to the real deposit rate is undoubtedly exaggerated. A government that mismanages one macroeconomic policy instrument is most likely to be following a variety of other growth-inhibiting macroeconomic policies. That the surge in inflation in 1984 and 1985 was not accompanied by declining growth cannot be attributed solely to the high real deposit rates of interest in these two years.

Realistic changes in deposit rates and rationalization of the taxation of financial intermediation suggest that other government-controlled prices were probably also adjusted in appropriate ways during those years. Previously rigidities of a variety of key prices, such as interest rates and exchange rates, made Turkish inflation a very costly affair. Perhaps Turkey has now learned to live with inflation as a far better alternative to pretending that it does not exist.

REFERENCES

Abe, S., M. J. Fry, B. K. Min, P. Vongvipanond, and T.-P. Yu. 1975. The demand for money in Pakistan: Some alternative estimates. *Pakistan Development Review* 14(2):249-57.

Aghevli, B., and M. Khan. 1977. Inflationary finance and the dynamics of inflation: Indonesia, 1951-72. *American Economic Review* 67(3):390-403.

______. 1978. Government deficits and the inflationary process in developing countries. *International Monetary Fund Staff Papers* 25(3):383-416.

Black, S. W. 1983. The use of monetary policy for internal and external balance in ten industrial countries. In *Exchange Rates and International Macroeconomics*, edited by J. A. Frenkel, 189-225. Chicago: University of Chicago Press.

Buffie, E. F. 1984. Financial repression, the new structuralists, and stabilization policy in semi-industrial economies. *Journal of Development Economics* 14(3):305-22.

Central Bank of the Republic of Turkey. 1982. *Annual Report*. Ankara.

______. 1984. *Uc Aylik Istatistik Ozetleri*. Ankara, March.

Dutton, D. S. 1971. A model of self-generating inflation: The Argentine case. *Journal of Money, Credit and Banking* 3(2):245-62.

Fry, M. J. 1971. Turkey's first five-year development plan: An assessment. *Economic Journal* 81(322): 306-26.

______. 1972. *Finance and Development Planning in Turkey.* Leiden:Brill.

______. 1978a. Alternative stabilization strategies from a model of short-run price and output fluctuations in Turkey. *METU Studies in Development* 5(18):21-36.

______. 1978b. Further investigation into Turkey's Phillips curve. *METU Studies in Development* 5(19):66-88.

______. 1978c. Money and capital or financial deepening in economic development? *Journal of Money, Credit and Banking* 10(4):464-75.

______. 1979. The cost of financial repression in Turkey. *Saving and Development* 3(2):127-35.

______. 1980a. Saving, investment, growth and the cost of financial repression. *World Development* 8(4):317-27.

______. 1980b. Money, interest, inflation and growth in Turkey. *Journal of Monetary Economics* 6(4):535-45.

______. 1981. Inflation and economic growth in Pacific basin developing economies. *Federal Reserve Bank of San Francisco Economic Review* (Fall):8-18.

______. 1982a. Models of financially repressed developing economies. *World Development* 10(9):731-50.

______. 1982b. Analysing disequilibrium interest-rate systems in developing countries. *World Development* 10(12):1049-57.

______. 1984. Saving, financial intermediation and economic growth in Asia. *Asian Development Review* 2(1):82-91.

______. 1986a. Terms-of-trade dynamics in Asia: An

analysis of national saving and domestic investment responses to terms-of-trade changes in 14 Asian LDCs. *Journal of International Money and Finance* 5(1): 57-73.

______. 1986b. Turkey's great inflation. *METU Studies in Development* 13(1-2):95-116.

Fry, M. J., and M. R. Farhi. 1979. *Money and Banking in Turkey.* Istanbul: Bogazici University Press.

Hemphill, W. L. 1974. The effect of foreign exchange receipts on imports of less developed countries. *International Monetary Fund Staff Papers* 21(3):637-77.

International Monetary Fund. 1977. *The Monetary Approach to the Balance of Payments.* Washington, D.C.: International Monetary Fund.

Johnson, H. G. 1972. The monetary approach to balance-of-payments theory. In *Further Essays in Monetary Economics*, by H. G. Johnson. London: Allen & Unwin.

Kapur, B. K. 1976. Alternative stabilization policies for less-developed economies. *Journal of Political Economy* 84(4):777-95.

Keller, P. M. 1980. Implications of credit policies for output and the Balance of Payments. *International Monetary Fund Staff Papers* 27 (3):451-77.

Kopits, G. 1984. Interest rate liberalization and demand for money in Turkey. International Monetary Fund DM/84/32. Washington, D.C.

Korteweg, P. 1978. The economics of inflation and output fluctuations in the Netherlands, 1954-1975: A test of some implications of the dominant impulse-cum-rational Expectations Hypothesis. *Journal of Monetary Economics* (supplement 8):17-79.

Krueger, A. O. 1974. *Foreign Trade Regimes and Economic Development: Turkey.* New York: National Bureau of Economic Research.

Laidler, D. 1978. Money and money income: An essay on the "transmission mechanism." *Journal of Monetary Economics* 4(2):151-91.

Lasker, D. M. 1983. Short-run independence of monetary policy under a pegged exchange-rate system: An econometric approach. In *The International Transmission of Inflation*, edited by M. R. Darby, J. R. Lothian, et al., 314-48. Chicago: University of Chicago Press for the National Bureau of Economic Research.

Lucas, R. E , Jr. 1973. Some international evidence on output-inflation tradeoffs. *American Economic Review* 63(3):326-34.

Mathieson, D. J. 1979. Financial reform and capital flows in a developing economy. *IMF Staff Papers* 26(3):450-89.

______. 1980. Financial reform and stabilization policy in a developing economy. *Journal of Development Economics* 7(3):359-95.

Ness, W. L. 1972. Some effects of inflation on financing investment in Argentina and Brazil. In *Financial Development and Economic Growth: The Economic Consequences of Underdeveloped Capital Markets*, edited by A. W. Sametz, 228-54. New York: New York University Press.

State Institute of Statistics. 1984. *Monthly Economic Indicators.* Ankara, February.

Taylor, L. 1983. *Structuralist Macroeconomics: Applicable Models for the Third World.* New York: Basic Books.

Uluatam, F. A. 1973. *Monetary Multipliers and a Self Generating Inflation Model: The Turkish Case.* Ankara: Turkish Republic State Planning Organization.

van Wijnbergen, S. 1982. Stagflationary effects of monetary stabilization policies: A quantitative analysis of South Korea. *Journal of Development*

Economics 10:133-69.

______. 1983. Credit policy, inflation and growth in a financially repressed economy. *Journal of Development Economics* 13:45-65.

6

Financial Liberalization and Savings in Turkey

LIBBY RITTENBERG

A key feature of the 1980 Austerity Program in Turkey was the promotion of domestic savings by means of financial liberalization. According to a growing body of literature stemming from the theoretical works of McKinnon (1973) and Shaw (1973), traditional monetary and fiscal stabilization tools become more effective if used in conjunction with financial reform. The argument is that financial repression, symbolized by negative real interest rates associated with nominally pegged interest rates during periods of inflation, leads to the withdrawal of funds from the banking sector. The reduction in real credit availability lowers actual investment and economic growth. A policy recommendation, therefore, is to free, or at least rationalize, interest rates. Because the interest elasticity of savings is assumed to be positive, higher real interest rates will stimulate both the savings rate and the investment rate (due to an increase in available credit) and hence growth.[1]

The purpose of this chapter is to examine Turkey's savings function to determine whether its structure changed between the pre-1980 and post-1980 periods in ways predicted by the literature on financial liberalization. Attention is focused on the role of positive real interest rates in promoting savings during the liberalization period.

The results indicate that (1) there was a substantial autonomous drop in the savings rate from 1982 onward, which may have been the result of shaken public confidence following the bankruptcy of the major brokerage houses; (2) increases in the real interest rate led to increases in the savings rate; and (3) the savings rate increased at a decreasing rate as the real interest rate rose. Thus, while negative interest rates discouraged savings in the 1970s, positive real interest rates in the 1980s had a much milder effect in terms of encouraging savings.

Two policy recommendations follow from this study. First, positive real interest rates are a necessary but insufficient condition for higher savings rates. This symbol of financial liberalization must be accompanied by the creation of orderly financial markets. Second, excessive positive real interest rate increases should be avoided because of their diminishing impact in terms of bringing forth additional savings. Beyond some point, higher interest rates will have an adverse impact on investment and growth.

A national savings model is specified and estimated in the first section. In the second section the same model is applied to private savings. The third section provides insight into the appropriate level of the real interest rate.

ESTIMATION OF THE NATIONAL SAVINGS FUNCTION

Following Fry (1979, 1980) and Giovannini (1983) the ratio of national savings to GDP was regressed on the rate of growth of real GDP, the level of per capita GDP (in logarithmic form), the ratio of foreign savings to GDP, the real deposit rate of interest, and the savings rate lagged by one year. The rationale for the inclusion of each of these variables is described in Mikesell and Zinser (1973). The coefficients of real income growth and per capita real income are expected to be positive. The inclusion of the foreign savings rate seeks to determine whether or not foreign savings may substitute for national savings.[2]

The real deposit rates used in the present study are simply realized rates rather than estimates of expected rates. Realized rates were also used by de Melo and Tybout (1986), and Mathieson provides theoretical support for this procedure. Mathieson argues that in economies with histories of rapid inflation ". . . expectations are less sticky because the cost of ignoring the future effects of current policy actions can be quite high. Under this rational expectations hypothesis, the expected rate of inflation will equal the actual rate of inflation . . . ." (1979:458).

Table 6.1 lists the regression results from the model for periods beginning in 1961 and ending in the years shown. Notice first that the real growth rate is never significant; it conforms with estimates obtained by Leff and Sato (1980) for countries with histories of macroeconomic instability. Second, the coefficient of per capita GDP is consistently positive and significant, while that of foreign savings is negative and significant. Thus foreign savings appear to substitute for domestic savings.

The troublesome coefficients are those estimated for the real deposit rate and the lagged savings rate. The former is never significant after 1979 while the latter is only significant after 1980. Whereas the structure observed by Fry (1979) appears to hold for the pre-1980 period, it breaks down after 1980.[3]

In order to account for shifts in the savings function in the post-1980 period, dummy variables were added to the equation. The results are shown in Table 6.2. Initially, a dummy variable was included for each year starting in 1980. Because the coefficients for the dummy variables in years 1982-85 were nearly identical, only one dummy is included for these years. In the first column all of the variables suggested for inclusion in the savings model have been used. In the second column, real income growth and the lagged savings rate were excluded because their coefficients lacked statistical significance.

Several important conclusions emerge. First, with the inclusion of the dummy variables, the coefficient of the real deposit rate is estimated to be positive and statistically significant. Also, its magnitude is nearly identical to that estimated for the pre-1980 period, indicating that savings do respond favorably to higher real interest rates as predicted by the literature on financial repression and liberalization. Second, there was an autonomous jump in the savings rate in 1980, and in 1981 the savings rate fell slightly. From 1982 to 1985 the magnitude of the drop was substantially higher and consequently is more worrisome.

The upward shift in 1980 probably results from error in measurement of the real deposit rate for that year as well as from the inception of liberalization.

TABLE 6.1 Parameter Estimates for the Savings Function before Taking Account of Structural Shifts

Data Base[a] Ends in	Estimates[b]						R^2
	c	g	y	f	r	s_{t-1}	
1977	-0.57 (-4.91)	-0.04 (-0.56)	0.18 (5.62)	-0.76 (-5.41)	0.15 (1.60)	0.06 (0.36)	0.90
1978	-0.62 (-4.74)	-0.03 (-0.30)	0.18 (5.04)	-0.68 (-4.39)	0.31 (4.03)	0.26 (1.54)	0.86
1979	-0.60 (-4.60)	-0.04 (-0.45)	0.18 (4.95)	-0.69 (-4.49)	0.27 (3.96)	0.20 (1.24)	0.85
1980	-0.29 (-2.25)	0.03 (0.22)	0.10 (2.61)	-0.50 (-2.57)	0.08 (1.42)	0.35 (1.63)	0.71
1981	-0.27 (-2.68)	0.04 (0.34)	0.09 (3.18)	-0.49 (-2.63)	0.07 (1.55)	0.38 (2.00)	0.72
1982	-0.17 (-2.15)	0.08 (0.75)	0.06 (2.74)	-0.46 (-2.39)	0.02 (0.72)	0.42 (2.20)	0.69
1983	-0.14 (-1.77)	0.14 (1.39)	0.07 (2.42)	-0.53 (-2.73)	-0.01 (-0.21)	0.39 (1.98)	0.66
1984	-0.11 (-1.58)	0.13 (1.35)	0.05 (2.31)	-0.50 (-2.65)	-0.01 (-0.43)	0.44 (2.36)	0.65
1985	-0.11 (-1.77)	0.13 (1.38)	0.05 (2.62)	-0.50 (-2.79)	-0.01 (0.46)	0.44 (2.53)	0.66

Sources: OECD *National Accounts 1960-85*, IMF *International Statistics*, Central Bank *Monthly Bulletins*, and IMF *International Financial Statistics*.

[a] Regressions begin in 1961

[b] D.W. Statistic fluctuated between 1.9 and 2.5.

Symbols:
- s = ratio of national savings to GDP
- c = constant term
- g = real GDP growth (expressed as proportion)
- y = natural logarithm of real per capita GDP
- f = ratio of foreign savings (i.e., current account deficit) to GDP
- r = real deposit rate of interest calculated as $[(1+i)/(1+p]-1$, where i = nominal deposit rate and p = rate of increase of CPI (all numbers expressed as proportions)

TABLE 6.2 Parameter Estimates for the Savings Function after Taking Account of Structural Shifts

Variable[a]	Estimates[b]	
c	-0.57 (-4.08)	-0.68 (-6.95)
g	0.02 (0.26)	
y	0.17 (4.47)	0.20 (8.69)
f	-0.70 (-4.61)	-0.78 (-6.02)
r	0.24 (3.28)	0.29 (3.74)
s_{t-1}	0.18 (1.14)	
Dummy variable equal to 1 for 1980	0.07 (3.04)	0.08 (3.74)
Dummy variable equal to 1 for 1981	-0.02 (-1.25)	-0.03 (-2.33)
Dummy variable equal to 1 for 1982-85	-0.08 (-3.61)	-0.10 (-6.07)
R^2	0.79	0.80
D.W.	2.22	1.94

[a]See Table 6.1 for sources and explanation of notation.

[b]All the variables suggested for inclusion in the model have been used in the first column, whereas in the second column those whose coefficients had very low t-statistics were excluded.

While the annual inflation rate exceeded 100 percent, most of the inflation occurred in the first half of the year. In the second half of the year interest rates were freed and savers were undoubtedly attracted. The sharp downward shift after 1981, however, may represent what Diaz-Alejandro (1985) referred to as an "unintended consequence of financial liberalization." His analysis of the cycle of financial repression-financial liberalization-financial crash, observed in several Latin American countries, can be applied to Turkey with minor institutional variations. For example, in July 1980 a private and virtually unregulated money market began to form in Turkey. The collapse of that market, which began in late 1981 and was completed by June 1982, destroyed public confidence and precipitated withdrawals from the banks, especially those whose certificates of deposit were marketed by the private moneylenders.[4] Indeed, the lack of recovery of savings four years later, as individuals returned to more traditional inflation hedges, such as gold and real estate purchases, provides an empirical estimate of Diaz-Alejandro's unintended consequences of financial liberalization.

The foregoing does not suggest that return to the days of negative real interest rates is appropriate. As shown in Table 6.2, higher savings are associated with higher real rates of interest. However, there is a strong sense of missed opportunity; the higher interest rates and the general financial environment appear to have been at odds in the post-liberalization period.

ESTIMATION OF THE PRIVATE SAVINGS FUNCTION

Since the financial repression literature actually posits a relationship between private savings and market variables, a separate savings equation was estimated using private savings as a fraction of private disposable income. In addition, real private disposable income replaced real GNP as a determining factor, the foreign savings rate was specified as a fraction of private disposable income, and the ratio of public savings to private disposable income was included to allow for consideration of the extent to which public and private savings are substitutes. While there is reason to believe that these data may be less reliable than the aggregate numbers, their consideration does provide a check on the parameter estimates of the previous section.

The regression results are shown in Table 6.3 and can be compared to the estimates reported in Table 6.2 for total savings. As before, in the first column all the variables suggested for inclusion in the model have been used, whereas in the second column those whose coefficients had very low t-statistics were excluded.

There is considerable agreement between the two sets of estimates in terms of overall fit, the signs of the coefficients, and their statistical significance. The only coefficient with a different sign is the real private disposable income growth rate; however, this variable is not statistically significant. Also, the coefficient of the dummy variable for 1980, while positive, is not statistically significant.[5]

Nonetheless, the results do seem to corroborate the conclusions of the previous section. In particular, as the financial repression literature predicts, real interest rates have a positive influence on private savings. Moreover, as before, there appears to have been a relatively small autonomous drop in the private savings rate in 1981 followed by a substantially larger drop in the 1982-85 period. Thus, the comments of the previous section concerning unintended repercussions of financial liberalization still seem appropriate.

THE SELECTION OF THE APPROPRIATE INTEREST RATE

An important issue of development policy is the appropriate interest rate level. In other words, how high is high enough given that beyond some level, investment and growth may be squeezed by less favorable terms of credit.[6]

The estimates shown in Table 6.4 attempt to answer this question. The regression uses the national savings rate as the dependent variable and allows for a nonlinear relationship between the interest rate and the savings rate. The overall fit of the data is improved, when compared to the results of Table 6.2, as indicated by the higher coefficient of determination. More important, the coefficient of the linear term is estimated to be positive and significant, while that of the quadratic term is estimated to be negative and significant. Thus, increases in the interest rate appear to lead to increased savings but at a decreasing

TABLE 6.3 Parameter Estimates for the Private Savings Function, 1961-85

Variable	Estimates	
c	-0.04 (-3.61)	-0.33 (-4.52)
g′	-0.07 (-1.47)	-0.06 (1.50)
y′	0.08 (4.23)	0.06 (5.91)
f′	-0.48 (-3.67)	-0.43 (-4.08)
p′	-0.24 (-1.52)	-0.17 (-1.29)
r	0.14 (1.82)	0.09 (1.99)
s_{t-1}	-0.05 (0.25)	
Dummy variable equals to 1 for 1980	0.02 (0.89)	
Dummy variable equal to 1 for 1981	-0.04 (-3.13)	-0.04 (-3.15)
Dummy variable equal to 1 for 1982-86	-0.08 (-3.54)	-0.07 (-4.53)
R^2	0.72	0.74
D.W.	2.01	2.16

Sources: Same as in Table 6.1 except for private savings, public savings, and private disposable income which are from the Turkish State Planning Organization.

Symbols:
- s′ = ratio of private savings to private disposal income
- c = constant term
- g′ = real private disposable income growth (expressed as a proportion)
- y′ = natural logarithm of real private disposal income
- f′ = ratio of foreign savings to private disposable income
- p′ = ratio of public savings to private disposable income
- r = see Table 6.1

TABLE 6.4 Parameter Estimates for the Savings Function Allowing for Nonlinear Relationship between the Savings Rate and the Real Deposit Rate of Interest

Variable[a]	Estimates
c	-0.66 (-7.62)
y	0.20 (9.50)
f	-0.67 (-6.08)
r	0.19 (3.18)
r^2	-0.75 (-3.44)
Dummy variable equal to 1 for 1980	0.16 (5.37)
Dummy variable equal to 1 for 1981	-0.04 (-3.39)
Dummy variable equal to 1 for 1981-85	-0.08 (-5.61)
R^2	0.87
D.W.	1.92

[a]See Table 6.1 for sources and explanation of notation.

rate.[7]

Table 6.5 shows the estimated change in the savings rate for various changes in the values of the real deposit rate. While 5-percent increases in the real deposit rate lead to increases in the savings rate of one percentage point or more when the real deposit rate

TABLE 6.5 Estimated Effects of Change in Real Deposit Rate on Savings Rate

r	s
-.30 to -.25	.030
-.25 to -.20	.026
-.20 to -.15	.022
-.15 to -.10	.019
-.10 to -.05	.015
-.05 to 0	.011
0 to .05	.007
.05 to .10	.004

is negative, similar increases in the savings rate when the real interest rate is positive are considerably more modest, on the order of one-half of one percent or less. Hence, because of the eventual detrimental effects of higher positive interest rates on investment and growth, I conclude that real interest rates should be held relatively low if growth is an objective.

CONCLUSIONS

A national savings function was estimated for Turkey over a period which covered the pre-1980 years of import-substitution-industrialization and the post-1980 years of stabilization and liberalization. The slope estimates were found to be stable over the entire period. However, following an initial autonomous shift upward in 1980, the function shifted downward for the 1982-85 period. This was assumed to have been caused by the collapse of the private money market in 1982 and the ensuing public panic which precipitated withdrawals of savings from the banking system. Thus the interest-rate policy and the financial environment appear to have been working at odds in the post-liberalization period. Despite higher real interest rates, shaken public confidence discouraged savings.

A similar function was estimated for private savings. The results essentially corroborated those obtained by estimating the national savings function. Most important, this function was also estimated to have shifted downward in the 1982-85 period.

Turkey has become another country to follow what Diaz-Alejandro (1985) described as a cycle of financial repression-financial liberalization-financial crash, typical of a number of developing countries. While these results do not suggest the desirability of a return to the days of extreme negative real interest rates, they do suggest that financial reforms must be carried out with extreme care. Cautioning against a free money-market and advocating an eclectic approach, Diaz-Alejandro wrote, ". . . even if one believed, à la Hayek, that the externalities and public good characteristics of the domestic monetary and financial system are negligible, one may conclude that the political, and social, infrastructure found in many developing (and developed?) countries conspires against the viability of such a pure laissez-faire financial system" (1985:18).

NOTES

1. Fry empirically verified a positive and statistically significant interest elasticity of savings for Turkey for the years 1957-77 and calculated the "cost of financial repression, that is, holding institutional interest rates below their equilibrium levels" to be about "half a percentage point in economic growth foregone for each percentage point by which the real rate of interest was held below its competitive, free market equilibrium level." (Fry 1979:134-35).

2. Of course, testing the relationship between the real interest rate and the savings rate relates to the importance of financial liberalization. Note that lagged saving allows for partial adjustments of savings to their desired levels.

3. The coefficient reported by Fry for the real deposit rate was 0.27, which is quite close to those shown in Table 6.1 for the periods ending before 1980.

4. See Gültekin and Inselbag (1985).

5. The magnitudes of some of the coefficient estimates, however, do vary somewhat between the national and private savings functions. In particular, the coefficient of the real deposit rate of interest is considerably lower in the latter case.

6. The real deposit rate reached 14 percent in 1983.

7. A similar regression was estimated using the private savings rate as the dependent variable. While the quadratic term was insignificant, the coefficient of the real deposit rate was much smaller initially.

REFERENCES

de Melo, J., and J. Tybout. 1986. The effects of financial liberalization on savings and investment in Uruguay. *Economic Development and Cultural Change* 34(3):561-87.

Diaz-Alejandro, C. 1985. Good-bye financial repression, hello financial crash. *Journal of Development Economics* 19:1-24.

Fry, M. J. 1979. The cost of financial repression in Turkey. *Savings and Development* 3(2):127-35.

______. 1980. Saving, investment, growth and the cost of financial repression. *World Development* 8(4):317-27.

Giovannini, A. 1983. The interest elasticity of savings in developing countries: The existing evidence. *World Development* 11(7):601-7.

Gültekin, B., and I. Inselbag. 1985. Financial markets in Turkey. Paper presented at the eleventh annual meeting of the Eastern Economic Association. Pittsburgh, March 21-23.

Leff, N. H., and K. Sato. 1980. Macroeconomic adjustment in developing countries: Instability, short-run growth, and external dependency. *Review of Economics and Statistics* 22(2):170-9.

Mathieson, D. J. 1979. Financial reform and capital flows in a developing economy. *IMF Staff Papers*

26(3):450-89.

McKinnon, R. I. 1973. *Money and Capital in Economic Development.* Washington, D. C.: The Brookings Institution.

Mikesell, R. F. and J. E. Zinser. 1973. The nature of the savings function in developing countries: A survey of the theoretical and empirical literature. *Journal of Economic Literature* 11(1):1-26.

Papanek, G. F. 1973. Aid, foreign private investment, savings, and growth in less developed countries. *Journal of Political Economy* 81(1):120-30.

Roe, A. R. 1982. High interest rates: A new conventional wisdom for development policy? Some conclusions from Sri Lankan experience. *World Development* 10(3):211-22.

Shaw, E. S. 1973. Financial deepening in economic development. New York: Oxford University Press.

7

Financial Markets in Turkey

IŞIK INSELBAG AND N. BÜLENT GÜLTEKIN

It is customary to describe the degree of development of financial markets in terms of allocational and operational efficiency. Financial markets are allocationally efficient when they channel surplus funds to the most productive and profitable uses. If the intermediation costs of transferring funds from investors to users are low, then markets are described as operationally efficient. Competition between instruments, institutions, and other financial participants form the essential elements aiding the market to approach both types of efficiency.

Currently, financial markets in Turkey lack both allocational and operational efficiency. Existing legislation and practices lead to segmentation in financial markets and restrict competition. This chapter describes the structure of financial markets in Turkey; it reviews developments during the 1980s, pinpoints the problem areas, and suggests some policy measures to solve these problems.

THE STRUCTURE OF MARKETS AND INSTITUTIONS

Turkey's financial system consists of a banking system, a capital market for bonds and stocks, and an unorganized money market. The banking system is dominant, as it is in most underdeveloped financial markets. It consists of the Central Bank, forty-six commercial banks (public and private), and four development banks.

Two of the development banks, State Investment Bank (SIB) and State Industry and Workers' Investment Bank

(SIWIB), are publicly owned. The SIB concentrates on financing State Economic Enterprises (SEEs) at subsidized rates. The SIWIB specializes in financing the "worker firms," which were established mainly through the participation of workers who live abroad. The two private development banks, the Industrial Development Bank (IDB) and the Industrial Investment and Credit Bank (IICB), serve the private industrial sector by providing medium- and long-term foreign exchange loans.[1]

The thirteen public commercial banks in existence were initially established to concentrate their activities in related sectors of the economy. Thirty-three commercial banks are privately owned. Of these, seventeen are either completely foreign or joint ventures.[2]

Commercial banking is highly concentrated. The assets of the four largest banks equal over half of the assets of the entire banking system. The largest nine banks control more than 80 percent of total deposits and are partially or wholly owned by major private holding companies. They also have a high level of participation in industrial and commercial firms.

The banking system is regulated by the Ministry of Finance and the Central Bank through a banking law, the critical regulation being in the area of interest rate controls. Until July 1980, for example, both deposit and credit rates were determined by the government or the Central Bank.[3]

The money and capital markets are rather small in comparison to the banking system. The bond market is dominated by government securities. In the 1980-82 period, for example, government bills and bonds and SIB issues constituted 85 percent of total bond issues in the primary markets. During the 1983-85 period this proportion rose to 98 percent. Government securities are marketed through the Central Bank and the Agricultural Bank. Bonds issued by the SIB are placed with pension funds that are government administered.[4] SIB in turn uses the proceeds of its bond issues in financing the SEEs. Since private pension funds are insignificant in Turkey, almost all of the sources of pension funds are channeled to the public sector.

The secondary bond markets are inadequate. Since long-term government bonds have been redeemable at par at the Central Bank or the Agricultural Bank, and since the majority of the bonds were sold with repurchase guarantees at predetermined prices in the corporate bond market, the need for a genuine secondary market that would provide liquidity has been limited.

The stock market has been and remains inactive. Supply and demand is limited in both primary and secondary markets. On the supply side, private corporations are reluctant to go public, and therefore they tend to favor debt rather than equity financing. Demand is limited because the rates of return on shares have not been competitive with those obtained from investment in such nonfinancial assets as gold, real estate, or durable consumer goods during low interest rate periods and in such financial assets as bank deposits and bonds during times of high interest rates. Perhaps the lack of competitiveness can be attributed to the small size and inadequacy of the secondary market in stocks.

RECENT DEVELOPMENTS IN FINANCIAL MARKETS

The structure of financial markets has remained virtually unchanged for long periods. Banks have remained dominant in the financial system despite some investors and borrowers (whose demands and needs had not been satisfied by the banks) moving to unorganized money markets with relatively small operations. Changes in the stock and the bond markets have been minor. Life insurance has remained undeveloped as an institution, with no active participation in Turkish capital markets, unlike insurance in developed countries. Pension funds have continued to flow to SEEs. Efforts to enact a law to organize and encourage the development of money and capital markets were unsuccessful through the 1960s and 1970s.

Deregulation During 1980-82 Period

Important developments in financial markets began with the inception of the January 1980 austerity program. As a first step, determination of deposit rates and credit rates on nonpreferential credit was liberalized in July 1980. Basic lending rates for preferential credit in areas like exports, agriculture, and certain categories of investments remained under the control of government as a tool for monitoring selective credit programs.

With the initiation of the free interest-rate policy, banks attempted to set deposit rates through gentleman's agreement. Initially, the major public banks felt the pressure of rising rates but chose not to comply. Brokerage houses of the unorganized money market took advantage of this situation by offering significantly higher rates to investors. At the same time, since the government failed to lift controls on corporate bond interest rates, corporate issuers started using the brokerage houses to market their bonds. These two factors led to a fairly large but unregulated money market.

Successive adjustments in the deposit rates offered by the banking system, coupled with decreases in the inflation rate, led to high, positive real interest rates. The banks began to transfer the increased cost of deposits to their commercial and industrial corporate clients through higher lending rates. Despite very high borrowing costs and due to a lack of institutions and legislation that would make equity more appealing than debt financing, companies continued to borrow to stay in business. In turn, this held demand for loans at high levels and prevented lending rates from falling.

Brokerage houses continued offering unusually high interest rates to attract investors. They offered certificates of deposit from banks and corporate bonds, but many preferred their own promissory notes and postdated checks.[5] Several brokers had difficulty in placing the funds they accumulated to earn sufficient returns to support promised interest payments and repurchase guarantees. Consequently, the majority of small brokers failed in December 1981. Most of the remaining brokerage houses failed to adjust to measures introduced by the government to regulate money markets. The bankruptcy of the largest brokerage house in June 1982 destroyed public confidence and the money market. It also led to withdrawals from banks, especially from the ones whose certificates of deposits were marketed through brokerage houses. The Central Bank had to provide funds to banks to prevent the crisis from deepening further.

The collapse was largely the result of interest rate deregulation, which increased promised rates above the inflation rate without establishing efficiency and an orderly functioning of the financial markets. Lack of well-established institutions, instruments, and procedures facilitated abuse of the tremendous public demand for financial investments as a hedge against inflation. If investors had been better informed about the instruments they were investing in through disclosure, credit rating, and investment counseling, perhaps the collapse could have been avoided.

Re-regulation of the Financial System, 1983-86

After the crisis in the money market, authorities attempted to stabilize the financial structure by supporting the banking system. Competition in deposit rates was restricted, use of certificates of deposits was discouraged, and controls on interest rates were reimposed. In December 1983, the Central Bank was again authorized to establish ceilings on deposit interest rates.

In May 1985, a new banking law was enacted, replacing the 1982 decree (which was initially introduced to reform the banking sector). The new legislation contained some provisions to address the structural weaknesses of the banking system, including essential provisions regarding the capital structure of banks, the protection of deposits through an insurance plan and deposit insurance fund, treatment of nonperforming loans, auditing, and a standardized accounting system. To promote competition on the lending side, the new law also tightened conditions regarding credit extended to individual customers.

The 1981 legislation of the Capital Market Law (CML) was another step to deal with the financial crisis. The law established the Capital Market Board (CMB) as a regulatory agency that was also responsible for organizational matters. The CMB was assigned the role of regulating, supervising, and promoting the primary and secondary capital markets. It was authorized to grant permission for new security issues and introduce new regulations concerning the capital markets. It was also given the authority to examine the financial positions of corporations (involved in the market) and nonbank financial institutions. The law made the first step toward introducing disclosure in the financial system, requiring corporations with a large number of stockholders to publish their financial statements. The CML also set some principles regarding the formation of nonbank financial institutions--underwriting corporations, investment trusts, and mutual funds.

Recent Developments

Over the last three years the authorities in Turkey introduced new procedures to promote deepening and widening of financial markets; therefore, they have encouraged the establishment of new institutions and financial instruments. In March 1984, Parliament enacted a law to encourage savings and public investments. It authorizes the government to issue Income Sharing Certificates (ISC) for public projects like dams, power stations, bridges, and highways. Funds raised through the sale of these certificates are accumulated to finance public investments.

At about the same time, a communiqué on special financial houses was issued, which led to the establishment of two joint ventures with Arab companies. These institutions issue Profit-Loss Sharing Certificates (PLSC).[6]

In May 1985, an auction system for the sale of treasury bills and notes was introduced and banks and securities firms were allowed to participate. In April 1986, an interbank money market in domestic currency began to operate. The Central Bank acts as an intermediary in this market, where banks are allowed to enter transactions in amounts related to the value of treasury bills and bonds used as collateral. The banks' use of government securities for this purpose as well as their ability to use them as a part of their liquidity reserves have made them the major investors in treasury bills and notes.[7]

While issuance and trading in government securities have been increasing rapidly, the growth of such activities in corporate securities has been much slower. This may be attributed partly to a lack of well-functioning secondary markets in corporate stocks and bonds. Since the Capital Market Law was mainly concerned with primary markets and initial offerings, in 1983 a law was enacted to regulate secondary markets. This decree gave CMB the authority to supervise and regulate stock exchanges, related institutions, and all secondary-market activities.

The Istanbul Stock Exchange (ISE) was reopened in January 1986. Secondary-market operations began to be carried out in the ISE and the over-the-counter market. However, off-board trading in listed securities was forbidden. Public sector securities (since they were not listed) were only traded outside the exchange. The trading volume in ISE is still low but increasing. The prices of traded stocks have risen dramatically since 1986. During 1986 the stock index rose nearly 70 percent, and during the first six months of 1987 the index more than doubled. However, it is still too early to assess the potential success of ISE.

Another new development in capital markets was to allow corporations (by the CMB) to issue commercial paper. Permission was given to development banks in 1986 and to industrial corporations in 1987. According to the procedures determined by the Board, joint stock companies could issue commercial paper if they had not incurred a loss in the previous year and were audited by external auditors, or subject to a bank guarantee and the CMB's approval. The immediate reaction to these developments has been favorable. Development banks raised 60 billion TL in 1986 and industrial corporations sold 52.3 billion TL worth of commercial paper during the first eight months of 1987. Note that the commercial-paper market is critical for the development of financial markets in Turkey since it provides competition for the banking system.

Despite significant measures to deepen and widen the financial system, it is still dominated by the banking system, and most of the funds invested in financial assets are still channeled to banks and the public sector. Some basic institutions and instruments that exist in more developed markets are still lacking or not operating effectively. An active stock market, investment banking houses, merchant banks, money-market funds, independent auditing, and credit rating are institutions badly needed. Insurance companies and pension funds need to be active participants in financial markets. Basic money-market instruments such as commercial paper and bankers' acceptances should become significant and permanent components of the financial system, and certificates of deposits should be revitalized.

POLICY MEASURES

Financial markets constitute a bridge between surplus and deficit units in the economy and provide a place for the determination of prices for future cash flows for both savers and users of funds. The role of a viable financial structure is to channel savings in the economy to the most deserving investment opportunities at the lowest possible cost. It is clear that the financial markets are far from this state in Turkey. The current financial structure is a simple one in which the government and the banking sector collude to force savings out of households and channel them into the government sector at subsidized rates and into the private sector with very high markups.

There are a number of policy measures that are interrelated and should be undertaken more or less simultaneously to improve capital markets in Turkey. Currently the most critical ingredient missing in Turkish financial markets is competition. Either by coincidence or by conscious effort, there is no effective alternative to commercial banks. The first step, therefore, is to encourage competition by developing new financial institutions and instruments.

Second, government intervention in the determination of interest rates should be abolished. It is not fair competition when the government sells tax-exempt bonds on the one hand and, on the other, forces the private sector to sell bonds at before-tax prices too low to allow a sufficient premium for the difference in risk and for payment of taxes from the interest income. Because of chronic budget deficits, the government sector is the largest user of funds, and authorities seem to wish to keep the cost of borrowing low by simply stipulating low interest rates.

Third, new financial institutions with underwriting and brokerage functions need to be developed to increase the allocational and operational efficiency in the primary and secondary markets.

It is also desirable to encourage money-market funds and related instruments such as commercial paper. Similarly, certificates of deposits are important money-market instruments, and regulatory obstacles to their issuance should be eliminated, even though revitalization might recall the chilling experience of the "bankers' panic of 1982." Allowing banks to issue certificates of deposit in July 1987 was a step in the right direction. Such money-market institutions and instruments will allow, at least, larger corporations to raise funds directly from the financial markets withouut the costly intermediation of the commercial banking system and will instill confidence among savers in the financial markets. Steps taken along these lines during 1987 have been encouraging.

An important consideration in creating new securities is to provide the freedom for market participants to decide on and create the types of instruments that are most suitable for investors. It is not reasonable to expect that financial innovations would come from regulatory authorities. Everybody's interests are best served if these agencies spend their energies in insuring full disclosure and prevention of fraud in the markets.

Two important issues involving the Turkish capital markets need immediate attention. First is the disclosure of all information necessary to make appropriate investment decisions by the suppliers of securities. Second is creation of a viable equities market.

The quality of information to the market is vitally important. There is a crying need for a standard accounting system, standard accounting practices, and independent auditors. The importance of information and the role of standard accounting practices cannot be overemphasized. Currently the CMB takes the responsibility of requiring standardized accounting statements and assumes the auditing function itself. With the growth of new issues, its staff will soon be inadequate to fulfill this function. Auditing can be best accomplished by independent auditors as in the United States.

Similarly, independent rating agencies are needed to certify the quality and risk levels of debt securities. Standardization is an important condition for the success of securities, and rating agencies would provide useful information in this process.

The importance of viable equity markets as a source of funds for firms is obvious, but equity markets are thin in Turkey. Perhaps the primary reason is the predominance of family owned private corporations. Under the current structure, it is doubtful whether successful privately owned corporations in Turkey would ever go public. Most larger corporations are under the umbrella of a holding structure and are integrated with their own commercial banks.

Development of equity markets is essential, not only in providing new funds to sustain economic expansion, but also in making possible healthy debt-equity ratios, thus improving the ability of enterprises to weather economic slowdowns more successfully. Current debt-equity ratios of Turkish corporations are very high by any standard, which is a legacy of the high inflationary era with interest rate ceilings and, thus, negative real interest rates. The losses resulting from restrictive monetary policies were obvious from the high rate of business failures.

Another important aspect of equity markets is more political than economic. It is important for the public to participate in the economic expansion of the country by owning an equitable portion of the national wealth. Accumulation of wealth in the hands of a few cannot be a desirable, or even a sustainable, economic policy.

In order to accelerate the development of equity markets, certain fiscal incentive and coercion plans, which have been successfully implemented in a number of countries, would be useful. Incentive schemes usually involve preferential treatment of publicly held corporations. In Korea, for example, privately owned corporations have a statutory tax rate (including defense and residence tax) of 51 percent, while publicly owned corporations have a tax rate of 38 to 44 percent depending on the degree of public ownership. Korea also instigated one of the most successful programs in the development of equity markets. The Ministry of Finance required that corporations beyond a certain size go public. If they did not comply, the statutory tax rate for these corporations was raised to 61.2 percent. As expected, such direct measures in Korea had a more immediate impact on equity markets than did more indirect measures used in other countries.

Other recommended measures on the supply side include the abolition of double taxation of corporate earnings, which are taxed first at the corporate level and then taxed at the second level as dividends at ordinary income tax rates for investors. These measures have two objectives: to make equity investment more attractive for investors by eliminating taxes on dividends and capital gains, and to make the after-tax cost of equity as attractive for corporations as the after-tax cost of debt. In the classical system of double taxation, debt financing is always more attractive than equity financing, assuming other factors are held constant. Measures to eliminate taxation of corporate dividends and capital gains have already started to increase the demand for stocks.

Several other important fiscal incentive schemes are on the demand side. These measures may be a set of direct and/or indirect methods. Direct methods include an outright deduction in the income tax liability of an investor up to a certain percent and/or amount of an investment in equities or in selected mutual funds investing in equities. Others include preferential tax treatment of income from gains or income from other assets or transactions. In Korea, for example, while there is no tax levied on dividend income or capital gains from equities, the capital gains tax rate on real estate transactions is about 50 percent.

There are certain principles to keep in mind when introducing policies to develop financial markets. First, it is always imperative to recognize that investors are rational and that they can distinguish between real rates of return and nominal rates and between before- and after-tax returns. Also, one should remember that investment in equities is riskier than most other forms of investment. Incentive policies should not aim to alter the after-tax risk-adjusted return characteristics across different securities.

Second, measures should be undertaken with clear, predefined goals designed, for example, to broaden the stock ownership of the general population, increase the flow of new equity finance, improve market liquidity, increase the number of publicly owned corporations, or achieve some combination of these aims. The cost of such incentive schemes in terms of revenue loss to the treasury should be carefully considered against expected benefits.

There is today an unusual opportunity to stimulate the capital markets in Turkey. The authorities are working on a program of privatization of state economic enterprises (SEEs). We strongly recommend that the sale of these institutions be planned so that the objectives stated above concerning widening and deepening the financial markets can be fulfilled as well. Trading these institutions' securities in the stock market, if their securities are well distributed to the public, would create a market with extraordinary breadth and depth unparalleled in similar economies. Some of these organizations are currently not economically viable. After reorganizing and restructuring, most of them, if they are managed with economic rather than political objectives, should be viable enterprises. The sale of

SEEs to the public will create an equities market in a remarkably short time period.

NOTES

1. These two institutions have been losing importance in the 1980s.

2. The relative importance of these foreign banks in the system has been increasing.

3. During the inflationary periods of 1974-80, interest rates were set well below inflation rates, leading to negative real rates of interest.

4. In fact, it is required that these funds be invested in those bonds.

5. Another novelty of the government's free interest rate policy was the introduction of certificates of deposit for the first time in Turkey.

6. Relative to ISC, the interest in these certificates has been smaller. While issues of ISCs in 1984, 1985, and 1986 have been 10, 140, and 220 billion TL respectively, issues of PLSCs have been only 0.45 and 0.85 billion TL in 1985 and 1986.

7. The volume of public-sector securities increased by nearly 500 billion TL in 1986 to total 3,273 billion TL and constituted 95 percent of all issues.

REFERENCES

Central Bank of the Republic of Turkey. *Annual Report.* Various issues. Ankara.

Çoşan, F. M., and H. Ersel. 1987. Turkish financial system: Its evolution and performance 1980-86. Research and Development Department, Capital Market Board. Ankara.

Gültekin, B., and I. Inselbag. 1985. Financial markets in Turkey. Paper presented at the eleventh annual meeting of the Eastern Economic Association. Pittsburgh, March 21-23.

Tekbaş, M. 1987. Sermaye piyasasi. *Banka ve Ekonomik Yorumlar.* Istanbul.

8

The Role of Foreign Investment in the Liberalization of the Turkish Economy

ASIM ERDILEK

Turkey's 1980 economic stabilization and liberalization program assigned a significant role to direct foreign investment (DFI). The new outward-looking, export orientation of the economy was expected to benefit greatly from larger capital and technology inflows via DFI. In order for this objective to be realized, Turkey's DFI environment, which had deteriorated badly in the late 1970s, had to improve substantially. Besides the favorable overall reorientation of the economy, several DFI-specific institutional and legal reforms occurred that were expected to make Turkey more attractive to foreign investors. These cumulative reforms gained renewed emphasis after Turgut Özal came to power as prime minister in December 1983.

This chapter focuses on the DFI-related issues of the last two years and examines their interaction with Turkey's economic liberalization program. Although the major focus is on DFI, portfolio foreign investment (PFI) will also receive attention in terms of its potential role in economic liberalization. The first section reviews recent trends in the role of DFI in less developed countries (LDCs). The second section examines the latest DFI-specific economic and legal reforms and their implementation in Turkey. The third section reviews the most recent data on DFI flows and stocks and explains the trends revealed by those data in terms of changes in the DFI environment. The final section provides conclusions.

RECENT TRENDS IN THE ROLE OF DFI IN LDC

The 1982 global debt crisis has brought forward the importance of DFI (foreign ownership with managerial control) as well as PFI (foreign equity or debt participation without managerial control) as alternative channels of capital transfer.[1]

In the 1970s, both private and public capital flows from more developed countries (MDCs) to LDCs largely took the form of short- and medium-term credits rather than DFI or PFI (Giersch 1986). In most LDCs, including Turkey (Erdilek 1982:228-29), DFI was regarded with misgiving and treated with ambivalence. PFI, on the other hand, could not play much of a role, even if it had been welcomed. Unlike DFI, PFI depends significantly on well-developed debt and equity markets and is more easily discouraged than DFI by currency inconvertibility and other forms of direct host-government intervention.

During 1973-83, the stock of DFI in non-oil LDCs, concentrated in a few higher-income Asian and Latin American host countries, rose in nominal terms from $47 billion to $141 billion, at an annual rate of 11.6 percent. In Turkey, the DFI stock increased from $0.4 billion to $1.2 billion, also at an annual rate of 11.6 percent. Turkey's DFI stock share among the non-oil LDCs remained unchanged at 0.85 percent. In 1983, the share of DFI in total gross external liabilities (defined as DFI stock plus total outstanding external debt) for all non-oil LDCs was 17.0 percent; for Turkey it was 6.4 percent (IMF 1985:42).

For most LDCs, the sources of fresh foreign-debt capital have dried up because of the global debt crisis. Many LDCs have been forced to rely much more heavily on DFI, not only as a source of fresh foreign capital (IMF 1986a:72), but also as a means of foreign-debt management, that is, for debt-to-equity conversion (IMF 1986b:16-17, 62-64). There has been, however, a problem: For the same reasons that foreign bankers are loath to extend fresh credit to indebted LDCs, many foreign direct investors have been reluctant to get involved.

Although in recent years LDC after LDC has liberalized its treatment of foreign investors, relaxing restrictions and offering incentives (IMF 1986b:71-72), the perception of high risks relative to expected returns on DFI has continued to spread.[2] During

1967-82, DFI in LDCs increased at an annual real rate of over 5 percent, peaking at about $15 billion in 1981; but it has stagnated at about $10 billion per annum since 1983 (in constant 1980 dollars). It is believed that ". . . foreign private investment cannot be expected to make up for most of the decline in other capital flows to the developing countries" (IFC 1986:10-11).[3]

In the case of Turkey, foreign private investment is expected to total $1,235 million during 1985-89 (T.C. Resmi Gazete 1984:13-14). Interestingly, that cumulative amount of foreign private investment was only 8 percent of the Plan's total required financing: $16,270 million. This meant that the Özal government planned to improve Turkey's DFI-total gross external liability ratio slightly, but it would still fall far below the average ratio for non-oil LDCs.[4]

The plan projected net inflows of foreign investment to rise from $135 million in 1985 to $325 million in 1989, at an annual nominal rate of 19.2 percent. In 1985, the actual net inflow was recorded at $95 million (OECD 1986:64), implying a realization rate of 70 percent. It should be noted that the balance of payments (BOP) data on foreign investment are likely to underestimate the total foreign investment activity, especially DFI.

Recently Turkey's chief economic planner evaluated the role of DFI as a source of external financing and explained its current relative insignificance as follows: ". . . even after six years of adjustment that includes a remarkable streamlining of the foreign investment process, (DFI) flows are still rather small, amounting to only a few percentage points of the total fixed capital investment. In other words, potential for further development in this respect seems to be enormous. Apparently, elimination of restrictions and establishment of a sound legal base are necessary conditions to induce such flows; a sufficient condition that is yet to be fulfilled in the eyes of some observers is the creation of market perceptions of a sufficiently stable economic environment" (Tigrel 1986:1-2).

This statement overemphasizes Turkey's unfavorable experience with DFI in comparison with that of several other LDCs, in assigning a rather limited future role to DFI. It is correct, however, in stressing that more than a liberal DFI policy is required to attract the attention of foreign investors. What really matters is the DFI environment of a host country, which "can be defined as the aggregate of the factors that motivate (DFI), that influence the interactions of (DFI) firms and the host government, and that determine the absolute levels and the distribution of the net gains from (DFI)" (Erdilek 1985:31). The DFI policy of the host government is only one of those factors. The Turkish DFI environment needs to improve further before Turkey can attract DFI on a significant scale.

DFI-SPECIFIC LIBERALIZATION DURING 1985-86

Since December 1983, when the Motherland Party government headed by Turgut Özal came to power, Turkey's DFI policy has become progressively more liberal. This liberalization gained momentum from 1985 to 1986 as the government realized that overall economic liberalization was not attracting as much DFI as was expected.

The January 24, 1980, program had assigned a major role to DFI because of DFI's expected net benefits in terms of (1) additional foreign savings to finance faster development and to create more employment, (2) additional direct and indirect foreign exchange receipts to relieve the balance of payments pressures, and (3) additional transfers of technology to increase the economy's productivity and international competitiveness. As shown in Erdilek (1982), Turkey had realized very few such benefits from DFI before 1980 because of perverse Turkish government policies.

The Özal government's most significant DFI-related action in 1984 was to transfer the authority of the Finance Ministry, based on Decree 17 under Law 1567, over many DFI firms to the Foreign Investment Department (FID) of the State Planning Organization (SPO). This unified, under Law 6224, the government's regulation of all DFI firms except those in the petroleum sector, which were regulated separately under Law 6326. It also gave those DFI firms that had operated under Decree 30 much more operational and financial flexibility.

In 1985, the most significant DFI-related government action was the enactment of Law 3218 on Free Trade Zones (FTZs). The major objective of this law was to promote export-oriented DFI in designated regions of the country, which were exempt from most provisions applying to DFI activity outside the FTZs but subject to certain restrictions. For example, in the FTZs all operations would be exempt from Turkish taxes (except for a small transactions tax) and would not be covered for ten years by Turkish labor laws. The law thus assured a decade of no strikes and no lockouts. On the other hand, all payments in the FTZs had to be made in Central Bank-designated hard currencies. The first FTZ was opened in Mersin in January 1987. One more, in Antalya, is expected to go into operation soon.

In 1986, Turkey's DFI policy was liberalized further (YASED 1986a). The addendum to Decree 86/10353, dated March 13, 1986, and based on Law 6224 and Law 1567, introduced three important changes:

1. It revoked the Foreign Capital Framework Decree 8/168 (dated January 24, 1980) with its restrictive and discriminatory provisions. As a result, (1) 100 percent foreign ownership became feasible for all foreign investors and in all sectors; (2) disincentives for majority foreign ownership disappeared; and (3) discriminatory minimum export requirements that had been imposed on DFI firms, but not on Turkish-owned firms, were eliminated.
2. It replaced the DFI-related provisions of Decrees 28 and 30 issued under Law 1567, thus eliminating fiscal discrimination against the DFI firms operating under those decrees in terms of customs duty exemptions and other tax incentives.
3. It broadened the FID's authority to screen and approve DFI applications up to $50 million, even with 100 percent foreign ownership, and increased the FID's overall flexibility to regulate all aspects of approved DFI projects. Projects with total DFI of more than $50 million still required the approval of the Council of Ministers. The FID's regulatory authority with respect to both DFI and PFI, under Decree 86/10353, was spelled out in detail by the SPO's Communiqué 1, dated May 25, 1986.

As for taxes, the Özal government has virtually eliminated the legally questionable provisions, if not the bureaucratic practices, that had discriminated against foreign investors for many years. This move was consistent with Özal's opposition to any discrimination against DFI firms: "From our point of view, there is no difference between local establishments and establishments with foreign capital. Our policy is toward eliminating such differences" (Özal 1986:21).

In 1986, Turkish personal and corporate income tax legislation was amended significantly by Law 3239 (YASED 1986b). The following changes resulted from that law and subsequent related decrees and communiqués: (1) Nonresident taxpayers (foreign investors in a Turkish company as well as Turkish branches of foreign companies) became eligible for investment tax credits; (2) corporate withholding tax rates on various income categories of nonresident taxpayers were reduced; (3) corporate withholding taxes, which were paid in addition to regular corporate taxes on distributed earnings, that discriminated against foreign investors were eliminated; and (4) salaries paid by nonresident taxpayer employers to either Turkish or foreign employees were exempted from personal income tax, if payments were made from foreign exchange earned outside of Turkey.

Turkey has already enacted no-double-taxation treaties with Austria, Italy, Jordan, Norway, South Korea, and West Germany. It has either reached or is expected to reach similar agreements with Belgium, France, Holland, Pakistan, Sweden, the United Kingdom, and the United States soon.

Turkey, unlike several other host countries, offers no special incentives to foreign investors that are not also available to Turkish investors. Until recently, foreign investors were in fact discriminated against in the implementation of the official annual investment and export incentives schemes. These incentives still largely consist of: (1) exemptions from customs duties and taxes on all imported capital goods and on those imported inputs required by exports, (2) investment tax credits and cash grants (as percentages of total fixed investment), and (3) tax rebates for exporters (as a percentage of value-added tax). It seems highly unlikely that Turkey will offer, at least in the near future, any special incentives to foreign investors that are not also available to Turkish investors.

The progressive liberalization of the Özal government's DFI policy during 1984-86, which considerably improved the country's DFI environment, continued to be criticized on several grounds:

1. The post-1980 DFI legal framework has been based primarily on government-issued decrees instead of being codified into laws enacted by the Grand National Assembly (GNA). Many foreign investors have urged the Özal government to consolidate its liberal DFI policy into a law so that they can have greater confidence in that policy's durability. The government has considered this request seriously as part of its DFI policy (T.C. Resmi Gazete 1984:22; DPT 1986:92) but has not acted on it yet. Domestic political calculations as well as constitutional considerations are believed to have caused inaction.
2. Certain loopholes in Turkish patent laws have remained a source of concern for some foreign investors, especially pharmaceutical, computer software, and seed development companies. The government has drafted a new patent law in conformity with the Berne and Paris International Patent Conventions, but it is yet to be enacted.
3. Foreign investors fault the government for failing to provide financial stability as the basis of an effective DFI policy. They find Turkey's inflation and real interest rates still too high and the chronic depreciation of the Turkish lira (TL) discouraging. Between 1980 and 1986, TL's cumulative depreciation against the U.S. dollar was close to 900 percent.

There were other DFI-specific legal and institutional developments during the last two years. In 1985, Turkey signed a bilateral investment treaty (BIT) with the United States for "the Reciprocal Encouragement and Protection of Investments." It was expected to be ratified by the Turkish GNA and the U.S. Congress. The BIT guarantees that investors on both sides will receive the national as well as the most-favored nation treatment, sets standards for prompt and free fund transfers, and provides clear access to international arbitration for investors involved in disputes when mediation fails. In 1986, the Turkish-U.S. Business Council, a private organization with official backing, was formed. One of its objectives is to promote U.S. DFI in Turkey.

Aimed at attracting DFI into power generation projects, the "construct-operate-transfer" scheme of the Özal government has been much discussed as an innovative idea but has not yet yielded results.

TABLE 8.1 Distribution and Funding of Authorized DFI in U.S. Dollars (Millions)

	Authorized DFI	NGCC[a] and CTLD[b] Converted into Authorized DFI	Share[c] of Converted NGCC and CTLD in total DFI (percentage)
1954-1979	228	-	-
1980	97	35	36
1981	338	300	89
1982	167	89	53
1983	103	27	26
1984	271	29	11
1985	235	19	8
1986	364	8	2
Total	1,803	507	28

Source: Unpublished State Planning Organization data obtained from the Association for Foreign Capital Coordination (YASED) and translated by the author.

[a]NGCC = nonguaranteed commercial credits.

[b]CTLD = convertible Turkish lira deposits.

[c]Calculated by dividing the third column by the second.

RECENT DFI TRENDS IN TURKEY

Since 1980, according to SPO data, there has been a relatively uneven but remarkable increase in both the interest (in terms of authorized DFI) and the activity (in terms of realized DFI) of foreign investors in Turkey. Relative to total authorized DFI during 1954-79, there was a surge in authorized DFI during 1980-86 (see Table 8.1). Although the initial spurt in

TABLE 8.2 Distribution and Funding of Authorized DFI in Turkish Lira (Millions)

Year	Number of Authorizations	Authorized DFI	Customs Duty Exemptions	Equity	Debt
1980	28	44,048	7,853	18,273	17,922
1981	66	68,522	12,826	31,603	24,093
1982	53	84,397	12,808	41,865	29,724
1983	59	127,617	32,917	48,896	45,804
1984	180	278,640	37,196	158,556	82,888
1985	246	244,472	18,136	155,686	70,650
1986	318	920,288	123,005	435,581	361,702
Total	950	1,767,984	244,741	690,460	632,783

Source: Unpublished State Planning Organization data from the Association for Foreign Capital Coordination (YASED) and translated by the author.

authorized DFI significantly reflected the less than voluntary conversion of nonguaranteed foreign commercial credits and convertible Turkish lira deposits into DFI, the more recently authorized DFI increases were much less dependent on such debt-to-equity swaps.

Foreign investor interest in Turkey rose during 1980-86, as evidenced by the number of authorized DFI projects and the current TL million total investment values of those projects (see Table 8.2). These projects were aimed at either building new capacity or expanding/integrating/modernizing existing capacities. Two other trends are worth noting:

TABLE 8.3 Distribution and Capital Share of Actual Direct Foreign Investment Firms

Year	Number of DFI Firms	Actual DFI (TL Million)	Total Capital of DFI Firms (TL Million)	Share of Actual DFI in Total Capital of DFI Firms (percentage)
1975	109	2,177	5,418	40.18
1976	106	2,318	5,771	40.17
1977	99	2,480	6,326	39.20
1978	97	2,818	7,945	35.47
1979	91	2,518	8,480	29.69
1980	100	9,642	28,390	33.96
1981	127	19,012	47,400	40.11
1982	170	43,646	100,196	43.56
1983	185	61,352	147,109	41.71
1984	267	117,902	254,775	46.28
1985	421	208,408	464,981	44.82
1986	610	302,909	707,164	42.83

Source: Unpublished State Planning Organization data obtained from the Association for Foreign Capital Coordination (YASED) and translated by the author.

1. The customs duty exemptions-total investment ratio declined sharply, in fact almost halved, between 1980-83 and 1984-86. This might be interpreted as indicating to some extent a lower relative risk perception under the Özal government by foreign investors. Of course, it could also be due to other factors such as changes in the nature of individual

authorized DFI projects.

2. The debt-equity ratio of authorized projects also showed a downward trend between 1980-83 and 1984-86. This might have resulted from the Özal government's relatively more determined efforts to keep real interest rates positive. Interestingly, the debt-equity ratios implied by Table 8.2 are all less than unity, averaging 0.6 during 1984-86. Erdilek (1982:55-57) found mostly rising debt-equity ratios for the DFI firms before 1980, which averaged 1.5 at their peak. During 1975-80, Turkish real interest rates were not only negative but also falling (TUSIAD 1986:57).

The number of actual DFI firms, after continuously decreasing during 1975-79, rose sharply during 1980-86 (see Table 8.3). The same was largely true of both foreign capital and total capital of DFI firms in current lira values. It is also worth noting that the share of foreign capital in total capital showed a definite downward trend before 1980 but jumped to and appeared to stabilize at a higher level afterward. The higher percentage of foreign ownership, still averaging less than 50 percent, might be explained partly by Turkey's more liberal DFI policy and partly by the increased confidence of foreign investors in Turkey's DFI environment.

The sectoral distributions of the actual DFI stocks in 1985 and 1986 are found in Tables 8.4 and 8.5. Between the two years several changes occurred:

1. Manufacturing lost some of its relative importance in terms of both the number of DFI firms and the value of foreign capital but still accounted for more than half of both.
2. Within manufacturing, food and drinks, chemicals, and transportation vehicles were the relatively more important sectors in terms of DFI capital.
3. Both agriculture and mining were relatively insignificant in terms of both DFI firms and DFI capital.
4. Services increased in relative importance at the expense of manufacturing. DFI in services, severely restricted before 1980, accounted for about 20 percent of the total DFI value in 1979, much of it in tourism (Erdilek 1982: 256) but grew rapidly

TABLE 8.4 Distribution of Actual DFI by Sector, 1985-86

Sector	Number of DFI Firms		Share in Total DFI (percentage)		Share of DFI in Total Capital of DFI Firms (percentage)	
	1985	1986	1985	1986	1985	1986
Manufacturing	202	235	56.70	51.20	36.57	34.65
Agriculture	7	12	2.92	2.90	43.72	47.39
Mining	4	6	0.39	1.08	75.98	53.81
Services						
Trade	123	224	5.01	5.98	75.98	75.68
Tourism	20	41	4.77	6.44	49.81	43.69
Banking	19	21	21.03	18.08	74.02	56.87
Land transportation	4	6	0.73	0.58	64.90	66.69
Maritime transportation	3	3	5.73	5.10	49.96	49.96
Investment finance	-	2	-	2.80	-	85.00
Other	39	60	2.68	5.79	73.43	65.77
Services total	208	357	39.98	44.80	65.68	57.76
Total	421	610	100.00	100.00	44.82	42.83

Source: Unpublished State Planning Organization data obtained from the Association for Foreign Capital Coordination (YASED) and translated by the author.

during 1980-86 to about 45 percent of the total DFI value in 1986. This increase clearly resulted from the much more liberal DFI policy toward services.

5. Within services, banking was relatively the most important sector but lost some of its dominance in terms of DFI capital.
6. Most of the increase in the number of DFI firms was claimed by the trade sector in services, which was relatively unimportant and largely unchanged in terms of its DFI capital.
7. The percentage of foreign ownership differed among manufacturing, agriculture, mining, and services. It was the lowest in manufacturing. It varied significantly among the different manufacturing sectors from less than 10 percent to slightly more than 75 percent. Among the relatively more important sectors, food and drinks, and chemicals

TABLE 8.5 Distribution of Actual DFI in Manufacturing, 1985-86

Sector	Number of DFI Firms		Share in Total DFI (percentage)		Share of DFI in Total Capital of DFI Firms (percentage)	
	1985	1986	1985	1986	1985	1986
Manufacturing						
Electrical/electronics	21	22	5.30	7.20	51.92	45.22
Machinery	15	15	3.81	3.35	35.76	29.16
Fertilizer	1	2	0.46	1.41	47.25	56.51
Textile & apparel	21	29	3.76	2.84	47.10	47.78
Chemicals	31	36	7.28	8.04	75.32	76.28
Glass	3	3	0.85	1.07	9.66	9.10
Automotive equipment	9	10	6.72	7.20	34.05	33.98
Food & beverages	27	36	11.84	9.47	53.61	51.83
Metal products	14	15	1.18	0.78	25.78	18.96
Nonferrous metals	3	3	0.60	0.44	15.46	16.46
Iron & steel	8	8	5.80	3.26	18.01	13.33
Plastics	4	8	0.34	0.52	24.92	37.85
Cement	1	1	0.36	0.25	14.16	14.16
Paper	5	6	0.83	0.53	48.06	40.18
Forestry products	7	7	0.55	0.38	29.36	29.36
Tires	4	3	1.77	0.83	55.79	50.83
Baked clay products	6	4	0.59	0.32	30.73	28.45
Automotive components	9	10	3.54	2.82	38.71	30.98
Aircraft	2	2	0.11	0.08	49.00	49.00
Other	11	15	0.90	0.33	46.56	39.82
Manufacturing Total	202	235	56.70	51.20	36.57	34.65

Source: Unpublished State Planning Organization data obtained from the Association for Foreign Capital Coordination (YASED) and translated by the author.

stood out with majority foreign ownership.

8. The foreign capital ownership percentage share was the highest but declining in services. Its variation among the different service sectors was not as marked as that among the manufacturing sectors.

In 1979, banking accounted for about 4 percent of the value of total DFI under Law 6224 versus about 20 percent during 1985-86. The number of DFI banks increased from only three (averaging 7 percent foreign ownership) in 1979 to twenty-one (averaging 57 percent foreign ownership) in 1986. In 1986, there were fifty-four banks in Turkey, including the DFI banks. At least two-thirds of the thirty-three banks without DFI, especially the larger ones, were directly or indirectly under state control.

The rapid entry of foreign banks into Turkey has had a significant effect on the banking sector as a whole, despite the fact that their activities have been rather limited in terms of both volume and market segment. Most DFI banks with U.S. and Western European parents, specializing largely in foreign trade financing, have been more profitable than domestic banks. Recently they have become increasingly active in investment banking (a very underdeveloped field in Turkey) by underwriting corporate issues for Turkish borrowers in international capital markets.

Foreign banks have not brought in significant amounts of financial capital and have concentrated their primarily wholesale business in a few market niches that offer them clearcut advantages over domestic rivals. The example of their superior know-how and vastly more efficient operations are having a strong effect on all banking in Turkey. Turkish banking, especially before 1980, was shielded from any effective price competition and thus allowed to remain highly inefficient.

There is no question that foreign banks have ushered in modern banking practices despite the still overregulated nature of Turkish banking. They have significantly participated in the recent development of the Turkish interbank money market, which is perhaps the only legal truly free domestic financial market.[5] Their important potential in the development of the country's spot and forward foreign exchange markets has not yet been realized simply because the government has not allowed these markets, along with the domestic money markets (except the interbank market), to function freely.

If the DFI banks were to enter, without many restrictions, into all segments of the business, including retail banking, and to compete head-on with their domestic counterparts, they would revolutionize the whole sector.[6] Full convertibility plus free floating of the Turkish lira, if and when it became a reality, would enable the DFI banks to integrate their

Turkish operations into their global businesses. Only then would the Özal government's hopes of making Istanbul the international banking center of the Middle and Near East be realistic.

The DFI banks, if allowed a greater role, would also serve as a strong attraction for nonbanking DFI firms in terms of both the general confidence factor and the banking requirements of those firms. It is well known that multinational banks and manufacturing firms from the same source country tend to expand their foreign operations sequentially due to interdependence. They rely as significantly on each other in overseas markets as they do in domestic ones.

CONCLUSIONS

This chapter examined some of the DFI-related developments in Turkey during the last two years in the context of that country's seven-year-old economic liberalization program. The expected role of DFI in economic liberalization was underscored in terms of DFI's importance as a source of (1) external capital with distinct advantages over foreign debt-based liabilities, especially in the shadow of the global debt crisis; (2) foreign technology essential to increasing productivity and international competitiveness; and (3) various linkages between the domestic and world economies toward greater openness and rationalization of the former.

The chapter documented and also tried to explain the relative surge in both interest and activities of direct foreign investors in the Turkish economy after 1980.[7] The Özal government's increasingly liberal open-door DFI policy and the relative overall liberalization of the economy were emphasized as the determinants of greater potential and actual involvement of foreign firms in Turkey.

The actual role recently played by DFI in the country's outward-oriented development, although still much less than expected, could not be studied rigorously in depth due to lack of data. Such a study would be essential in testing the hypothesis that host-country benefits from DFI are primarily determined by the rationality of its own economic policies.[8]

Despite the recent DFI-specific and DFI-related economic and institutional reforms intended to make the country more attractive to foreign investors, Turkey does not yet have unique advantages as a host country. The outlook for its economy is evaluated cautiously by foreign investors (OECD 1986:41). Its DFI environment still suffers from serious disadvantages in terms of both economic and political instability compared to many other LDCs against which Turkey has to compete for the attention of increasingly risk conscious and selective multinational firms.

In reality, Turkish economic liberalization falls short of official claims about its scope and durability. Its scope is still severely limited by the Turkish lira's inconvertibility and several other forms of direct government intervention that prevent the market mechanism from allocating resources efficiently.[9] Its durability is in doubt due to both the government's own unstable policymaking and the uneven pace of the economy's development.[10] These two factors are, of course, interrelated with political instability, which also weighs heavily in the minds of foreign investors.

In short, for Turkey's efforts to attract a much greater volume of foreign private capital, ". . . the going may not be smooth for several years to come, perhaps until the rescheduled debts have been repaid in 1989 and the structural adjustment policies have had time to show their full effects" (OECD 1986:41). Political stability would remain an indispensable requirement, especially in light of the general election in 1987, further amendments to the 1982 Constitution, and the successor to President Evren in 1989.

Notwithstanding these short- and medium-term problems, Turkey's long-term attractiveness to DFI and the potential role of DFI in the Turkish economy's development deserve emphasis. Farsighted and patient DFI policies actively directed at promoting Turkey as a host country promise significant results. But the most effective way to attract DFI is to have a relatively open and stable economy. Then DFI requires no special incentives.

NOTES

1. See IMF (1984:136-44) for the technical distinction between DFI and PFI.

2. It is said good advice is required in two situations: before entering a third marriage and before

investing in an LDC.

3. See also IMF (1985:41) for data on DFI flows during 1960-82.

4. According to IMF (1986a:72), for the market-borrower LDCs, DFI flows represented 14 percent of the foreign borrowing requirement in 1980 but 30 percent in 1984.

5. In this market, which is the counterpart of the U.S. federal funds market, banks trade very short-term funds with each other at supply and demand determined rates.

6. That is unlikely to happen simply because many of the domestic banks could not survive the fierce competition.

7. Despite that surge, however, in 1985 authorized DFI was only 4.7 percent of the actual national gross fixed investment. According to past trends, one would expect less than half of the authorized DFI to be realized.

8. YASED (1986c) provides some empirical support for that hypothesis, based on 1980-82 aggregate data for DFI in manufacturing, in terms of improved export performance and overall contribution to the BOP.

9. Also, Turkish manufacturing is still heavily protected by high tariffs and surcharges.

10. The latter is clearly not independent of the former.

REFERENCES

DPT (State Planning Organization). 1986. *1986 Yili Programi* (1986 Annual Progam). Ankara.

Erdilek, A. 1982. *Direct Foreign Investment in Turkish Manufacturing: An Analysis of the Conflicting Objectives and Frustrated Expectations of a Host Country*. Tübingen: J.C.B. Mohr.

______. 1985. The dynamics of the foreign direct investment environment in Turkey. In *Political Risks in International Business: New Directions for Research, Management and Public Policy*, edited by T. L. Brewer. New York: Praeger.

______. 1986. Turkey's new open-door policy of direct foreign investment: A critical analysis of problems and prospects. *METU Studies in Development* 13(1-2):171-91.

Giersch, H. 1986. *The International Debt Problem: Lessons for the Future*. Tübingen: J.C.B. Mohr.

International Finance Corporation. 1986. *Annual Report 1986*. Washington, D. C.: International Finance Corporation.

International Monetary Fund. 1984. *Balance of Payments Manual*. 4th ed., Washington, D.C.: International Monetary Fund.

______. 1985. *Foreign Private Investment in Developing Countries*, Washington, D.C.: International Monetary Fund.

______. 1986a. *International Capital Markets*. Washington, D.C.: International Monetary Fund.

______. 1986b. *International Capital Markets*. Washington, D.C.: International Monetary Fund.

Organization for Economic Cooperation and Development. 1986. *Turkey--Annual Economic Survey*. Paris: OECD.

Özal, T. 1986. *Speech to YASED*. Istanbul: YASED.

T. C. Resmi Gazete. (Official Gazette of the Turkish Republic). 1984. *Besinci Bes Yillik Kalkinma Plani (1985-1989), Birinci Bolum* (Fifth Five-Year Development Plan, First Part), Ankara, 23 July.

Tigrel, A. 1986. *An Overview of the Turkish Economy*. Istanbul: YASED.

Turkish Industrialists' and Businessmen's Association, TUSIAD. 1986. *The Turkish Economy 1986*. Istanbul.

YASED (Association for Foreign Capital Coordination). 1986a. *Foreign Capital Legislation in Turkey*. Istanbul.

_______. 1986b. *Turkiye'de Yabancilarin Vergilendirilmesi* (Taxation of Foreigners in Turkey). Istanbul.

_______. 1986c. *Contribution of Foreign Investment to Turkish Economy*. Istanbul.

9

External Debt and Economic Performance in Turkey

DANI RODRIK

Since 1982, much of the developing world has been engulfed in a debt crisis whose resolution still seems far off. Turkey's performance during this period has been clearly anomalous. Riding high on an export boom, Turkey has emerged as a favored borrower in international capital markets and has managed to engineer a relatively high rate of economic growth, reaching nearly 8 percent in 1986.[1] In fact, ever since the 1970s Turkey's relationship with international credit markets has been consistently out of step with the rest of the developing world's. Turkey experienced its debt crisis in 1977-78, well before Mexico, Brazil, Argentina, and other leading debtor nations that experienced difficulties after the second oil shock. Before 1982, debt renegotiations undertaken between Turkey and its creditors involved the largest sums ever to be rescheduled. By 1982, just as commercial banks were reducing their Latin American lending to a trickle, Turkey was ready to re-enter private capital markets. Since then, its economic performance has been clearly superior to that of other heavily indebted countries.

Turkey now presents the single most important case of "life after debt." Its relative success in the 1980s has given rise to three interpretations. The multilateral lending agencies--the World Bank and the IMF--stress the "market-oriented" reforms undertaken since 1980 and especially the role of more realistic exchange rate policies, trade liberalization, higher domestic interest rates, and rationalization of the state-owned enterprises. In this particular vision, Turkey emerges as a successful Baker Plan country before the Baker Plan. A second strand of thought, common with the Turkish intelligentsia, emphasizes the role of domestic politics and the repression of workers' rights during this period. While not denying that particular economic reforms were instrumental in achieving success on the external front, this view highlights the internal social and political costs of the transformation and questions whether it is sustainable in the longer run. Finally, a third strand, potentially complementary to both of the above, emphasizes a number of fortuitous circumstances. Chief among these were the fall of the Shah in neighboring Iran, which triggered an avalanche of aid from strategic-minded OECD governments, and the Iran-Iraq War, which created a thriving export market for Turkish goods in these countries.

This chapter is a review and interpretation of some of the salient aspects of Turkey's experience with foreign debt since the early 1970s. In comparative perspective, this experience raises two important questions. First, why did Turkey get into a debt crisis after the first oil shock rather than the second one as has been the pattern? My argument here will be that between 1975 and 1977 Turkey relied heavily on a form of foreign borrowing that was intrinsically destabilizing. As I will explain, the infamous "convertible Turkish lira deposit scheme" of the period provided ever increasing incentives for overborrowing by the private sector. Hence the precocious nature of Turkey's debt crisis.

The second question is why Turkey's experience following the crisis offers such a sharp contrast to other debtor nations, which have struggled unsuccessfully since 1982. Here, my argument will be two-fold. On the one hand, Turkey has been the beneficiary of exceptionally advantageous treatment on the part of OECD governments, in terms of both debt relief and new capital flows. This has reduced the squeeze on the current account of the balance of payments. On the other hand, various export-promoting measures put in place since 1980 (including large, real exchange rate depreciations and overt subsidies) together with favorable market developments in the Middle East, have allowed imports to rise alongside reductions in the non-interest current account deficit. Thanks to both,

TABLE 9.1 Current Account Balances, 1972-77
(Percentage of GNP)

	1972	1973	1974	1975	1976	1977
All LDCs	-1.7	-1.3	-2.3	-4.2	-2.8	-2.6
Oil-importing LDCs	-1.5	-1.1	-3.9	-4.3	-2.6	-2.1
Turkey	0.3	2.4	-2.2	-5.1	-5.4	-7.1

Sources: World Bank (1985:17) and Central Bank.

the Turkish economy of the 1980s has not only avoided import compression but has also experienced a steady increase in the import ratio, thereby setting the stage for a healthy recovery.

THE CAUSES OF THE DEBT CRISIS OF 1977

The proximate cause of the crisis of 1977 was the sharp and continuous deterioration of the current account balance after 1973. It is customary to blame this outcome at least partly on the oil shock of 1973-74 and its consequences. According to Balassa's calcula- ations (1984), the balance-of-payment cost of the external shocks in 1974-76 amounted to -7.5 percent of GNP in Turkey.[2] This is higher than the average of -4.9 percent for all developing countries in Balassa's sample; furthermore, the figure for Turkey rises to roughly -9.2 percent if allowance is made for the reduction in workers' remittances from abroad (Rodrik 1986). But while Turkey was one of the countries hardest hit by these shocks, it was hardly alone. Even with the remittances effect added in, Balassa's figures show nine countries (out of twenty-four) with more severe external shocks than Turkey.

The external shocks of the mid-1970s do not go far in explaining the anomalous behavior of the Turkish current account. Turkey's experience was different from other developing countries in this respect (see Table 9.1). The situation in Turkey deteriorated sharply after 1973, as current account surpluses were rapidly transformed into deficits which kept on growing. Other oil-importing developing countries exhibited a similar, if less marked, increase in deficits in 1974 and 1975, which was followed by an improvement in 1976-77. Hence, the distinctive aspect of the Turkish experience was that the current account, once in deficit, never recovered. In turn, the requisite capital inflows became progressively larger.

What lay behind these deficits? In a purely accounting sense, their counterpart was a growing public-sector deficit. Of the rise in net external borrowing of 9.1 percentage points (as a share of GNP) between 1973 and 1977, 8.4 percentage points (or 92 percent) are accounted for by the deterioration of the public-sector balance and 0.7 percentage points (8 percent) by the decrease in private net savings. The predominant use made of foreign savings was investment rather than consumption. Around 76 percent of the increase in net foreign borrowing was accounted for by the rise in the national investment ratio from 18.1 percent (of GNP) in 1973 to 25.0 percent in 1977.[3] Foreign savings were ultimately channeled into the public sector and into domestic capital accumulation. This was clearly not a case of foreign borrowing to finance consumption.

While the capital inflows were used to spur investment, public-sector investment in particular, little of the foreign borrowing in this period was undertaken directly by the public sector. Throughout 1974-77, only a tiny share of the public-sector borrowing requirement was financed by direct external borrowing by the central government or by public enterprises.[4] Instead, foreign funds were brought in by the domestic private sector and channeled to the public sector via the banking sector. In effect, the private sector acted as intermediary between the foreign lenders and the government. This is a crucial part of the debacle that followed, so it is important to see how it occurred and what the consequences were.

The current account deficits of the period were financed in large part by a rather innovative form of foreign borrowing called the "convertible Turkish lira deposit" (CTLD) scheme. From practically zero at the beginning of 1975, these CTLDs rose to account for 48.9 percent of all short-term debt and 21.7 percent of all debt by the end of 1977.[5] In principle a liability of the private sector, the CTLDs were effectively socialized in a consolidation arrangement with foreign banks in the aftermath of the debt crisis in 1979.

The critical flaw of this scheme was that it provided domestic borrowers with blanket protection against exchange risk. The system worked as follows. Foreign banks, typically lured by Turkish businessmen, were allowed to open foreign exchange accounts with Turkish commercial banks. Their return on such deposits included a healthy margin over the analogous rates in Euromarkets--these margins were sanctioned and regulated by the Turkish authorities--as well as large front-end fees illicitly paid by the domestic entrepreneurs who brought them in. The commercial banks would turn over the foreign exchange to the Central Bank and receive credit with the Turkish lira equivalent of the deposit. The Central Bank could then use the foreign exchange to finance imports while the commercial banks used their new liquidity to make loans to the businessmen who had played the initiating role. In all this, neither the domestic private banks nor the eventual borrowers bore any exchange risk. The Central Bank provided the additional payments necessary when the Turkish lira depreciated against the foreign currencies involved--mainly Deutsche marks (DM) and Swiss francs.

The consequences of the CTLD scheme were devastating. The exchange guarantee provided Turkish borrowers with an implicit subsidy on foreign borrowing equal to the expected rate of depreciation. The ex post subsidy was the ex post rate of depreciation. As long as expectations were even vaguely "rational," this implied that the greater the magnitude of the exchange-rate disequilibrium, the larger the subsidy. In fact, the CTLD scheme proved so profitable that many entrepreneurs simply transferred funds abroad through the black market and brought them back in under the guise of foreign deposits, reaping the subsidy in the process.

The borrowing process after May 1975--when the expanded CTLD scheme was first introduced--can now be visualized as a vicious cycle. By 1975, the Turkish lira was already overvalued as a consequence of the lack of any serious adjustment to oil shock effects. The private sector had an incentive to overborrow abroad since the private costs of borrowing fell short of the social cost. This process further worsened the current account, making the current exchange rate even more overvalued. The private cost of foreign borrowing dropped, and the cycle continued. Such was the incentive to borrow under this scheme that the front-end fees paid by Turkish entrepreneurs to foreign banks eventually rose to more than 20 percent (Kafaoglu 1986:70). With spread and front-end fees included, the social marginal cost of foreign funds (denominated in DM) must have been at least 20 percent toward the end of 1976, implying a real interest rate of 15-16 percent. It is hard to envision that the real return to the marginal investment in Turkey at the time was anywhere near this figure.[6]

There can be little doubt that Turkey overborrowed in the aftermath of the first oil shock. Why is no mystery. Through the exchange guarantee, the private sector was motivated to borrow as much as possible, as quickly as possible. The closer the impending crisis, the more profitable it became to borrow. The fact that foreign borrowing ended up financing an investment boom by the public sector rather than a consumption spree by the private sector could not forestall the ultimate crisis.

CONSEQUENCES OF THE CRISIS

Once the Central Bank started getting into payments arrears by the middle of 1977 and foreign lenders withdrew, Turkey found itself in a full-fledged debt crisis. For more than two years, the economic policies followed by the various governments in power were insufficient to extricate the country from the crisis. Despite two IMF standby arrangements and various adjustment programs, the foreign exchange situation remained acute. The break came in 1980. In January of that year, the most drastic measures to date were announced, including a very large devaluation and steep price hikes for public enterprise products. During the same year, the OECD countries came through with a $1 billion special assistance package. In September 1980, the civilian government, beset by internal violence, was replaced by a military regime.

By what criteria should Turkey's adjustment experience after the debt crisis be evaluated? The performance of other developing countries after 1982 provides a natural benchmark for comparison. Table 9.2

TABLE 9.2 Post-Crisis Comparisons

	Real GDP Growth	CA Def. (Percentage of GNP[a])	CA Def.[b] (Percentage of GNP[a])	Import & NFS (Percentage of GNP[a])	Export & NFS (Percentage of GNP[a])	Inf.	Exchange Rate[c]	Public Sector Deficit[a]
				Turkey				
1974-77 average	7.6	4.9	4.4	13.7	6.2	19.9	100.3	7.1
1978	4.3	2.6	1.9	9.5	5.8	52.6	100.2	7.9
1979	-0.6	2.1	1.3	9.7	5.7	63.9	89.5	8.9
1980	-0.1	5.5	4.4	15.0	7.2	107.2	117.4	9.9
1981	4.7	3.5	1.5	16.5	10.9	36.8	121.0	3.7
1982	4.3	2.2	-0.5	17.4	14.6	25.2	140.2	5.0
1983	4.1	3.5	0.7	19.1	15.4	30.6	146.4	5.3
1984	5.8	2.8	-0.4	22.9	19.5	52.0	152.0	7.9
1985	4.3	1.9	-1.4	27.1	21.5	40.0	152.8	5.1
				Seventeen Highly Indebted Countries				
1978-81 average	3.9	3.7	1.5	16.2	14.8	58.9	92.8	4.8
1982	-0.5	5.9	0.8	16.1	15.3	80.5	89.0	8.2
1983	-3.0	1.9	-2.8	14.8	17.6	145.0	102.5	7.5
1984	1.9	0.1	-4.8	13.6	18.5	168.4	104.8	7.2
1985	2.6	0.1	-4.2	13.0	17.2	146.7	111.7	n.a.

Sources: For Turkey OECD, SPO, and own calculations; for others Choksi (1986).

[a]Percent of GDP for countries other than Turkey.

[b]Non-interest current account deficit.

[c]1974 = 100 for Turkey; 1978 = 100 for others.

displays some of the relevant data for Turkey and for a group of seventeen highly indebted developing countries. Several important conclusions emerge from the comparison.

First, in the wake of the crisis Turkey experienced a collapse in output growth very similar to that experienced by the other countries since 1982. Since 1981, however, the Turkish economy has been going through a healthy recovery. Part of the contrast with other countries has to do with the less accentuated retrenchment in Turkey on the current-account front. The average current-account deficit in Turkey in 1978-85 has been 3.0 percent (of GNP), more than three times the 0.7 percent for other countries in 1983-85 (see Table 9.2). The same pattern persists in the non-interest current account. In Turkey, the non-interest current account has been in surplus since 1982 on average, but at a much lower rate than has been the case in other highly indebted countries. Clearly, Turkey has been the recipient of proportionately larger capital inflows in the aftermath of its debt crisis than have other countries.

Second, Turkey's experience with exports has been astonishingly successful. Prior to the debt crisis, Turkish exports of goods and nonfactor services (as a share of GNP) stood at 6.2 percent, distinctly lower than the corresponding figure of 14.8 percent for the other countries. By 1985, the Turkish figure had jumped to 21.5 percent, leaving behind the modest gain of a total 17.2 percent experienced by the other countries. As the figures on import ratios show, this increase in exports has allowed a vast expansion of imports from the trough reached in 1978. The contrast with the progressive import compression after 1982 in the other countries is striking.

Third, following the burst in inflation in 1978-80, Turkish policy has been successful in stabilizing prices since 1981. The stabilization of inflation, together with an active exchange-rate policy, has allowed a vast real depreciation of the Turkish lira, on the order of 50 percent since 1977. On average, other developing countries have so far been unable to achieve gains in competitiveness of such magnitude. The progressive depreciation of the currency is no doubt at least part of the reason for the export boom mentioned above.

Finally, there has been some modest amount of fiscal adjustment in Turkey since 1981. As Table 9.2 shows, since 1981 public-sector deficits have hovered in the 3.5 to 5.5 percent range (with the exception of 1984), down from the previous range of 7 to 10 percent. By curtailing domestic demand, this has also contributed to the rise in exports.

To summarize, the Turkish adjustment experience differs from that of most other heavily indebted countries since 1982 in two key respects: (1) the relatively larger amount of financial flows made available to Turkey since the debt crisis; and (2) the superior export performance of the Turkish economy following the reforms of 1980. Both of these aspects have contributed to the recovery of the 1980s by allowing imports of intermediate and capital goods to expand. The next two sections examine capital inflows and export performance in further detail.

CAPITAL INFLOWS SINCE THE DEBT CRISIS

After the crisis of 1977, Turkey was shut out of private capital markets and was unable to raise any new loans from commercial banks until 1982. In 1978 and 1979 the consequence was a forced retrenchment of the current account and a buildup of payments in arrears. The current account deficit halved as a percentage of GNP, going from 4.9 percent in 1974-77 to 2.4 percent in 1978-79 (see Table 9.2). The mechanism by which the deficits were reduced was a rising rate of inflation as shortages of imported commodities developed, which cut the real expenditures of groups whose incomes were nominally sticky, principally workers and peasants (Rodrik 1986). In the meantime, however, the government undertook a series of debt renegotiations of an unprecedented size. Between 1978 and 1981, $9.8 billion of foreign debt was rescheduled, amounting to 70 percent of Turkey's total debt (exclusive of liabilities to international organizations) at year-end 1981. Of this, $5.5 billion (56 percent) was debt owed to OECD governments and $2.8 billion (29 percent) to commercial banks.[7]

Aside from this major relief operation, after 1979 Turkey also benefited from a coordinated effort on the part of Western governments to prop up the economy. The effort might have been forthcoming in any case, given the strategic importance of Turkey in NATO and its position in the Middle East. But the rescue package was also clearly influenced by events in neighboring Iran. The fall of the Shah in 1979 highlighted the value of a stable, friendly government in that particular hotspot of the world for the Western Alliance. Between 1979 and 1981, $1.5 billion was poured into the Turkish economy under OECD auspices as special assistance. In addition, during the same period the IMF and the World Bank lent $1.2 billion and $1.0 billion, respectively. These sums not only allowed the economy to weather the second oil shock but also provided an important breathing space in which to carry out the reforms of the early 1980s. Such flows allowed the current account deficit to jump to 5.5 percent (of GNP) in 1980 in the wake of the second oil shock.

In taking a closer look at the overall financing of the current account after 1977, it is useful to separate two subperiods, 1978-81 and 1982-85. This is convenient for two reasons: First, as the re-entry into private capital markets after 1982 indicates, the two subperiods exhibit different characteristics with respect to capital flows; second, and more mundane, the presentation of the balance-of-payments tables prepared by the Central Bank has been changed since 1982, with the consequence that it is difficult to present disaggregated flows on a consistent basis for the entire period.

Data on total financing needs in the first subperiod is calculated thus: The requisite financing is taken to be the sum of the current account deficit and amortization payments on medium- and long-term debt (both calculated on the counterfactual premise that no debt relief has been granted). This financing requirement amounts to $12.0 billion over 1978-81 (see Table 9.3). Clearly, the major role in closing the gap was played by debt relief (29 percent of the total), official bilateral lending (26 percent), and international organizations, mainly the World Bank and the IMF (22 percent). Short-term and private inflows played a miniscule role, in contrast to their prominent position until 1977. As these numbers reveal, it is hard to downplay the role of official and multilateral balance-of-payments assistance during this period. This is an important respect in which the Turkish post-crisis experience diverges from the common pattern after 1982.

Data on financial flows in the second subperiod, 1982-85, reveal some interesting comparisons (see Table 9.4). Debt relief in this later period played a much reduced role, accounting for 19 percent of the accumulated financing need of $12.3 billion and had no part at all by 1985. The same pattern is also evident for special OECD assistance. On the other hand, the greater reliance on private flows exhibits itself in the larger role played by short-term capital. Among the short-term inflows, two are of major importance: (1) Credits obtained by domestic commercial banks (denoted

TABLE 9.3 Financing of the Balance of Payments, 1978-81
(In Millions of U.S. Dollars)

	1978	1979	1980	1981	1978-81	%
Non-interest current account	-676	-403	-2270	-476		
Interest payments (before relief[a])	-489	-1010	-1138	-1443		
Current account balance (before relief[a])	-1165	-1413	-3408	-1919		
Debt repayment (before relief[a])	-451	-945	-1556	-1185		
Total financing	1616	2358	4964	3104	12042	100.0
Debt relief[a]	295	924	1450	850	3519	29.2
Interest	100	464	470	250		
Principal	195	460	980	600		
Multilateral lending (excl. IMF)	236	390	507	655	1788	14.8
of which: IBRD	173	280	313	454		
IMF (net)	213	11	422	268	914	7.6
Bilateral lending	356	751	1078	894	3079	25.6
of which: special assistance under OECD auspices	0	225	996	315		
Other[b]	516	282	1507	437	2742	22.8
of which: short-term credits	421	194	216	-212		
change in reserves	-187	76	-512	-263		

Sources: Central Bank, World Bank, and OECD.

[a]Refers to debt relief granted by OECD consortium.

[b]Includes short-term credits, change in reserves, DFI, and errors and omissions.

by "DMB" in Table 9.4) from private capital markets abroad; and (2) so-called Dresdner Bank accounts with the Central Bank. Between 1983 and 1985, the Central Bank also managed to raise $1 billion in syndicated bank loans.

The rising importance of private capital inflows is ample testimony to the newfound confidence in Turkey's

TABLE 9.4 Financing of the Balance of Payments, 1982-85
(In Millions of U.S. Dollars)

	1982	1983	1984	1985	1982-85	%
Non-interest current account	630	-387	179	740		
Interest payments (before relief)[a]	-1565	-1511	-1586	-1753		
Current account balance (before relief)[a]	-935	-1898	-1407	-1013		
Debt repayments (before relief)[a]	-1602	-1996	-1684	-1858		
Total financing	2537	3894	3091	2871	12393	100.0
Debt relief[a]	750	1000	580	0	2330	18.8
Interest	100	70	0	0		
Principal	650	930	580	0		
Long-term capital	980	677	1148	1159	3964	32.0
of which: project credits	754	508	733	923		
Short-term capital	81	1033	36	1650	2800	22.6
Public sector, net	-2	844	-189	328		
of which: Dresdner	344	433	528	400		
DMBs, net	69	93	66	1171		
Other sectors, net	14	96	159	151		
Exceptional financing	902	622	1002	676	3202	25.8
IBRD (SAL)	265	213	381	126		
USAID (loan)	400	64	85	0		
OECD	82	145	39	0		
Central Bank loan	0	200	300	500		
Other	155	0	197	50		
IMF	133	112	-141	-255	-151	-1.2
Other	-309	450	466	-359	248	2.0

Sources: Central Bank, World Bank, and OECD.

[a]Refers to debt relief granted by OECD consortium.

creditworthiness. Between 1983 and 1985, commercial banks undertook $1.9 billion of (net) new lending to Turkey (Watson et al. 1986). Notice, however, that this number is not particularly large: It amounts to around 19 percent of the total financing need in that period. "Net transfers" from abroad have been negative in this subperiod.

Turkey's success in reentering international capital markets notwithstanding, the growing reliance on short-term capital flows raises important questions. The stock of short-term debt has increased from $2.2 billion in 1982 to $6.6 billion in 1985, and its share in the total has doubled from 12.3 percent to 26.5 percent (see Table 9.5).[8] This trend is worrisome insofar as it implies that long-term debt is retired by converting it into short-term debt. In principle, the maturity of debt matters little in a perfectly rational world. But a preponderance of short-term debt clearly increases a country's susceptibility to confidence crises.

Further information on the composition of short-term liabilities can be gleaned from the information in Table 9.5. By 1985, the single most important item had become the Dresdner Bank scheme, amounting to 40 percent of all short-term debt. The purpose of this scheme is to channel the savings of Turkish workers abroad to Turkey. Essentially, the Dresdner Bank acts as an intermediary between the *Gastarbeiter* (guest workers) and the Turkish Central Bank, to which deposits made in Germany are transferred. This has been a successful mechanism with which to make use of the enormous savings potential of Turkish migrant workers. The presence of these migrants acts as a source of balance-of-payments support not typically available to other heavily indebted countries.[9]

In one important respect, however, this scheme is problematic. In order to attract such funds, the Central Bank has had to offer very high interest rates. As of the summer of 1986, the interest rates on two-year deposits were 12 percent on dollar deposits and 11 percent on DM deposits (prior to January 1985, these rates had been 14 percent for all currencies). This implies a spread of 4 to 5 percentage points over the London interbank borrowing rate (LIBOR), vastly in excess of the average for new borrowing by non-oil developing countries, which stood at 0.71 percentage

TABLE 9.5 External Debt, 1978-85 (In Millions of U.S. Dollars)

	1978	1979	1980	1981	1982	1983	1984	1985
Total External debt	14399	14223	16315	16861	17619	18391	21288	25012
Long-term debt	7223	7235	13835	14667	15455	15352	16782	18395
Multilateral organizations (incl. IMF)	1896	2474	3398	3857	4531	4916	5434	6103
Bilateral credits	4212	4370	5983	6712	7115	6566	7305	8013
(OECD)	3871	3976	5253	5901	6146	5613	6168	6776
Commercial banks[a]	487	3464	3436	3257	3229	3262	3693	4014
Private lenders	356	359	1018	841	580	608	350	265
Short-term debt	7176	3556	2480	2194	2164	3039	4506	6617
Public sector	1894	1104	1448	1161	1104	1737	2663	3755
of which: Dresdner Bank	363	344	365	473	817	1251	1778	2678
Bankers' credits	333	18	10	-	-	65	195	432
Overdrafts	341	244	254	69	48	164	417	376
Private sector	5282	2452	1032	1033	1060	1302	1843	2862
of which: CTLDs[b]	2860	617	543	473	585	647	61	18
Suppliers' credits[c]	1560	1400	-	-	-	-	-	-
Acceptance credits	862	435	377	230	276	318	703	1093
Pre-export financing	-	-	112	330	199	254	414	609
FX deposit accounts	-	-	-	-	-	83	544	724

Source: Central Bank.

[a]Includes rescheduled CTLDs from 1979 on.

[b]Non-rescheduled CTLDs

[c]"cash against goods."

points over LIBOR throughout most of 1986.[10] Notice that the highest spread witnessed for rescheduled debt in the present crisis has been 2.25 percentage points. On paper, then, the Turkish economy would be better off by simulating a debt crisis and rescheduling part of its debt than by servicing its liabilities at such rates.

For the moment, most of the interest earnings on these accounts appears to be redeposited, which is not surprising given the high yields. But even the semblance of a run on these accounts (if some reversals from Özal's policies become likely, for example) could prove ultimately disastrous.

EXPORT PERFORMANCE AND ITS DETERMINANTS

The availability of foreign inflows, as discussed in the preceding section, was an important factor in igniting the recovery of the Turkish economy since 1980 but probably not as important as export performance. The export boom in this period has been rather miraculous for a country long steeped in the traditions of export pessimism. The success on this front has played a key role in attracting commercial-bank lending since 1982, as well as allowing a healthy dose of export-led growth.

Official export statistics tell an impressive story. From around $2.5 billion in 1979, exports have steadily increased to $8 billion in 1985 in an external environment not particularly receptive. Two transformations came with this increase. First, the share of manufactured goods increased from 36.0 percent in 1980 to 75.3 percent in 1985, with a corresponding decline in the share of agricultural products. Second, the share of Middle Eastern and North African markets in total exports increased from 17.8 percent in 1980 to 41.9 percent in 1982, eventually declining to 33.0 percent by 1985. It is fair to say that this export boom has been the clearest success of the adjustment program of the 1980s.

What have been the determinants of the boom? Several factors are frequently cited. First, the Iran-Iraq War has created an important market for Turkish manufactured goods in the two belligerent countries; the war has been the predominant source of expansion for exports to the Middle East. Second, the government has followed a clearcut policy of export promotion, reflected in both an active exchange-rate policy and explicit export subsidization. As can be seen in Table 9.2, the real exchange rate has depreciated fairly steadily since 1980, such that the real value of the Turkish lira in 1985 stood 50 percent lower than in 1978-79. In addition, the ad valorem equivalent of export subsidies has amounted to more than 20 percent (Milanovic 1986). Third, relatively restrained monetary and fiscal policies in the early 1980s reoriented entrepreneurs toward foreign markets. Fourth, trade liberalization may have had its usual general-equilibrium effect of promoting exports. Finally, part of the export boom may have been the consequence of overinvoicing on the part of Turkish exporters keen on obtaining subsidized credit or tax rebates (the two most important categories of export subsidization). According to the last interpretation, much of the boom could be fictitious.

It is difficult to assess the precise effect each of these might have had, but an effort is necessary since so much hinges on the continuation of strong export performance. To begin with, we can rule out two of the factors cited above. It is unlikely that the restraint on domestic demand per se had much to do with exports. The reduction in real expenditures was sharpest in 1978-80, a period which was not characterized by success on the export front; moreover, exports skyrocketed in 1981 just as domestic demand was starting to recover. While the recovery was at least partly export led, depressed domestic demand on its own had been insufficient to boost foreign sales in the previous period. Similarly, it would be hard to sustain the case that trade liberalization had much to do with exports. The major break in the trade regime came in late 1983, a full two years after the export takeoff.

How about the so-called fictional exports? Here it is possible to provide some broad orders of magnitude by analyzing partner-country data. Given the unreliability of import data in some of the leading Middle Eastern countries, I have limited the analysis to OECD countries only. It is likely that this will lead to some understatement of the extent of overinvoicing. Casual empiricism suggests, however, that the bulk of "fictional" exports went to OECD countries. The method followed here consists of comparing recorded Turkish exports to the OECD with the recorded imports of OECD countries

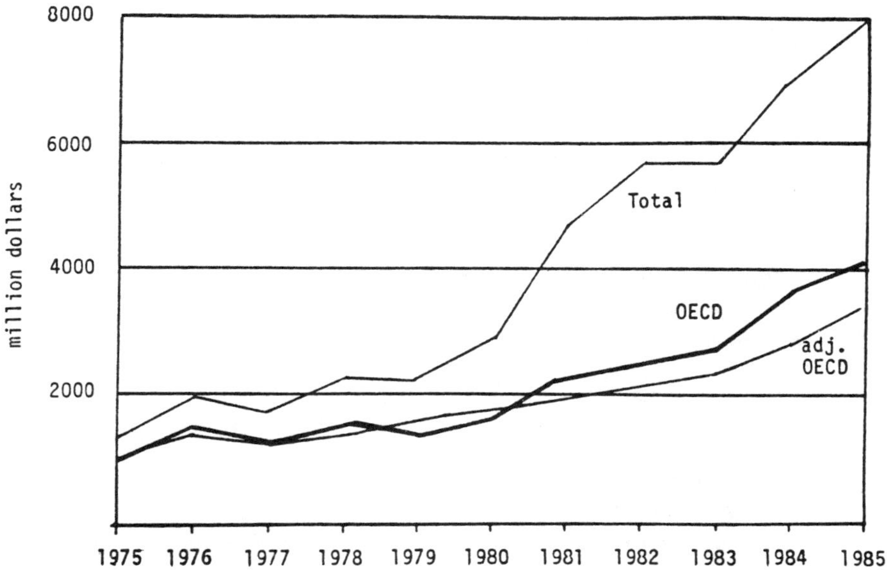

Figure 9.1. Export performance, 1975-85.

from Turkey, after adjusting the latter for freight and insurance costs.[11] The difference between the two sets of figures can be taken to indicate the magnitude of overinvoicing [or underinvoicing if recorded Turkish exports fall short of (adjusted) recorded OECD imports].

The results of the exercise are presented graphically in Figure 9.1. The top line represents total recorded exports during 1975-85. The two other lines track exports to OECD countries, as officially recorded in the Turkish export statistics and as calculated from the OECD import statistics in the manner indicated above. Notice that until about 1978 the latter two lines match each other fairly well. During 1979-80 there is evidence of a moderate amount of underinvoicing (around 5 percent). After 1981, however, the presence of substantial amounts of overinvoicing is unmistakable. The extent of overinvoicing averages 16 percent during the 1981-85 period, compared to nearly zero percent during the 1975-80 period. Such "fictional" exports appear to have been concentrated in a few countries, and in Germany in particular. Further disaggregation shows, for example, that recorded exports to Germany were at least 45 percent higher than actual exports in 1984. As export subsidies were phased out starting in 1985, some of the overinvoicing appears to have been reduced, as Figure 9.1 also reveals.

How worrisome this overinvoicing should be is not clear. To the extent that they brought in foreign exchange which otherwise would not have been brought in, export subsidies worked just like a one-time devaluation. As long as the shadow price of foreign exchange exceeds the "effective" rate on exports (inclusive of the subsidies), overinvoicing provides net benefits to the economy. On the other hand, to the extent that the subsidies have simply rechanneled foreign exchange receipts--from workers' remittances to "exports"--the net effect of the program would be very low. The generally downward trend in recorded workers' remittances since 1981 suggests that a considerable amount of substitution has taken place. In addition, the overstatement of actual exports leads to undue optimism as to the extent of structural change the Turkish economy has undergone in the 1980s: The presumably beneficial reallocation of resources toward export-oriented sectors has been much slower than official statistics would indicate.

After eliminating the "fictional" component of exports, we can analyze the determinants of the remaining portion. Here, some of the factors previously cited--exchange-rate policy, Iran-Iraq War, and so forth--stand out. In order to ascertain the relative importance of the various forces at work, I have estimated some export equations which link the volume and value of trade (adjusted for overinvoicing or underinvoicing) with the real exchange rate, export subsidies, foreign demand, credit policy, and a dummy variable which captures the effects of the war. The results are portrayed in Table 9.6. This regression should be viewed as a reduced-form relationship between the right-hand side variables and the dollar value of exports; both supply and demand effects are included.[12]

The results of this econometric analysis are satisfactory. The real exchange rate has the expected positive sign and is statistically significant. So is the industrial production index for the industrial countries, representing the state of foreign demand. The domestic real credit variable, standing in for the monetary stance and the buoyancy of domestic demand, has the expected negative sign but is statistically

TABLE 9.6 Determinants of Export Performance

Independent variable: Export value, adjusted for overinvoicing (monthly average, millions of dollars)

	Constant	LRXTWPEW	LIPDC	LRCRED	DUMMY
Coefficient	-3292.98	269.88	601.31	-50.65	159.58
t-statistic	(-5.72)	(2.88)	(5.04)	(-0.76)	(4.60)

Time period: 1975:I - 1984:IV

R^2 = 0.91 RBAR^2 = 0.90

Durbin-Watson: 2.22

SSR: 79278.74 SEE: 47.59

Key LRXTWPEW: Export-weighted real effective exchange rate, lagged once (in logs).

LIPDC: Industrial production index for industrial countries (in logs).

LRCRED: Real domestic credit stock (in logs).

DUMMY: Dummy variable; 0 until 1981: I (inclusive), 1 thereafter.

insignificant. Finally, a dummy variable which presumably reflects the effect of the Iran-Iraq War as well as any other changes after 1981 not captured in the regression, is also highly significant. In the initial runs, I had also included the export subsidy rate as a separate variable on the right-hand side. But its coefficient was negative and statistically insignificant, so I have excluded it here. On the whole, with an adjusted R-squared of 0.90 and relatively satisfactory test statistics, the regression does a good job of tracking actual exports.

The good fit obtained allows us to attempt a rough decomposition of the sources of the export boom. Since the regression covers the period through 1984, I concentrate on the years between 1979 and 1984. As Figure 9.1 shows, the major break in the pattern of export growth takes place in this period. Between 1979 and 1984, recorded exports increased by $4.6 billion. Adjusting for overinvoicing in 1984 and underinvoicing in 1979, the actual increase in exports was $3.6 billion, that is to say, 21 percent of the recorded increase in exports was fictitious. The rest can be decomposed using the slope coefficients in Table 9.6. My rough estimates based on these are as follows. Approximately $1.6 billion (35 percent) of recorded exports is due to the real depreciation of the exchange rate over this period. Another $0.5 billion (10 percent) is due to increased foreign demand from industrial countries. The expansion in real credit appears to have had a small negative effect on exports of about $0.1 billion (-3 percent). Finally, $1.9 billion (42 percent) is due to the Iran-Iraq War and other changes after 1981, captured by the dummy variable.[13]

These calculations, rough as they are, highlight the critical roles played by three variables: (1) the export subsidies which led to the unprecedented over-invoicing of the 1980s; (2) the active real-exchange rate policy, which has not only maintained competitiveness but has steadily increased it; and (3) the Iran-Iraq War and possibly the overall change in the domestic policy environment around 1981 (the dummy variable cannot distinguish between the two). In the future, only the second of these will remain a genuine policy option. But continuing real depreciations have their costs, too. First, they tend to depress real wages. There has been a drastic drop in real wages since the heights reached in 1977, and there is a limit to how far this process can go without engendering disastrous long-term consequences. Second, in an economy where capital-account flows have been liberalized, real depreciations imply levels of real interest rates higher than in the rest of the world. This depresses domestic investment and increases the fiscal burden of interest charges. Third, and perhaps most important, real depreciations entail substantial capital losses on foreign debt, and these have to be financed eventually out of the public-sector budget. With a debt GNP ratio of around 0.5, a 10 percent real devaluation amounts to an increase in the real public deficit of 5 percent of GNP.

CONCLUDING REMARKS

While the Turkish "success story" can be qualified in a number of ways as the discussion here has illustrated, it is hard to avoid the conclusion that Turkey's performance has been vastly superior to that of other highly indebted countries. I have stressed two critical aspects of the story. First, the financial support of OECD governments and of multilateral agencies played a key role in alleviating the squeeze on the current account in the initial stages of the recovery. Second, a combination of export-promotion policies and good luck led to an export-led growth process. While comparing Turkey to other countries, it is worth remembering that in 1978-79--before heavy OECD involvement and the reforms of 1980--Turkish performance did not look much different from the typical pattern after 1982.

The prospects for the future are uncertain. The "easy" stage of export promotion, based on an increasing rate of utilization of existing capacity, is now almost certainly over. The export boom can continue only if private investment in tradables revives. The experience of 1986 revealed how brittle the external equilibrium really is. A domestic, demand-led boom has played havoc with the trade balance, despite the reduction in oil prices, and exports have fallen in absolute terms. The export trend appears to have been restored in 1987 but only after the reintroduction of many export subsidies in late 1986. The challenge for the future will be to maintain the recovery without damaging overall confidence in the state of the economy. Any semblance of a confidence crisis could set the economy back several years by bringing private capital inflows to a virtual standstill.

NOTES

The work reported here is partially based on joint research with Merih Celasun in the context of the NBER Project on Developing Country Debt. Research assistance was provided by Isabel Marshall and Diana Edge. I am grateful to my discussant, Osman Ataç, for helpful comments.

1. According to a 1984 survey of debt swap arrangements, Turkey's creditworthiness was ranked behind only three East Asian countries (Malaysia, South Korea, and Thailand). See *Euromoney* (1985).

2. This figure is the sum of terms-of-trade and export-volume effects (Balassa 1984).

3. These numbers are calculated from statistics put together by the State Planning Organization. See

Table 7 in Rodrik (1986).

4. Table 8 in Rodrik (1986).

5. The debt totals mentioned here exclude arrears and overdue payments on CTLDs in 1977.

6. For further discussion and evidence on the CTLD episode, see Rodrik (1986).

7. The rest was mainly nonguaranteed debt owed to foreign exporters which had not been paid on time.

8. These figures overstate somewhat the share of short-term debt, as some of the Dresdner Bank accounts (included here as short-term debt) have a maturity exceeding one year. Excluding these, the share of short-term liabilities has risen from 10 percent (1982) to 18.8 percent (1985), with a further increase in 1986 to 22.1 percent.

9. Of course, if Latin American flight capital could be persuaded to return, the effect would be the same.

10. Table 21 in Watson et al. (1986).

11. I have assumed that these costs add 8 percent to the f.o.b. value of exports from Turkey.

12. The dependent variable, value of exports, is made up of a price and a volume term. For the purposes of estimating true elasticities it would be preferable to use export volume. My intention here is simply to describe a reduced-form relationship, without getting too much into the precise linkages involved.

13. These numbers are calculated using the estimated coefficients in Table 9.6 and multiplying them by the change in the average value of the right-hand side variables between 1979 and 1984. The percentages do not add up to 100 percent since the regression equation slightly underestimates average exports in 1979 and slightly overestimates them in 1984.

REFERENCES

Balassa, B. 1984. Adjustment policies in developing countries: A reassessment. *World Development* 12(9):955-72.

Choksi, A. 1986. Adjustment with growth in the highly indebted middle-income countries. CPD discussion paper 1986-36. Washington, D.C.: The World Bank.

Euromoney, February 1986.

Kafaoglu, A. B. 1986. *DCM Dosyasi.* Istanbul.

Milanovic, B. 1986. Export incentives and Turkish manufactured exports 1980-1984. World Bank Staff Paper 768. Washington, D.C.: The World Bank.

Rodrik, D. 1986. Macroeconomic policy and debt in Turkey during the 1970s: A tale of two policy phases. John F. Kennedy School of Government Discussion Paper 157D, Harvard University.

Watson, M., et al. 1986. *International Capital Markets.* Washington, D.C.: International Monetary Fund.

10

Problems and Prospects: A Commentary

TEVFIK F. NAS

Each of the previous chapters is an in-depth analysis of one aspect of Turkey's 1980-87 liberalization experience. When examined together, they provide important linkages which lead to several generalizations with consistent policy implications. These generalizations are examined in the first section. The second section provides a brief description of two potential further extensions of the liberalization process. The summary and concluding remarks follow in the final section.

THE IMPACT OF POST-1980 LIBERALIZATION STRATEGY: A COMBINED SUMMARY

Turkey's recent liberalization strategy incorporated aspects of gradualism with long-term expectations. The measures introduced as part of the 1980 stabilization and liberalization package included gradual liberalization of the import and export regimes, promotion of export-oriented industrialization, nominal devaluations, and gradual relaxation of foreign exchange restrictions. The main goals of the package were to achieve low rates of inflation and unemployment, attract foreign direct investment, and attain a favorable growth rate and balance of payments. Turkey's efforts on these fronts are analyzed in Chapters 1 and 2 by Şenses and Odekon, respectively.

While the overall outcome of this strategy has yet to materialize, the prevailing view among the authors of this book is cautiously optimistic. According to Conway, the frequent devaluations of the period seemed to improve the trade deficit but at the same time caused lower output and higher inflation. The improvement in the trade deficit, Conway argues, may have resulted from reduced investment rather than expenditure switching. During the 1980-84 period, investment declined because of higher real interest rates, and inflation rose because of increases in the final good and imported input prices.

Conway also reports on the favorable effects of reduced tariffs on imported inputs. Apparently this form of trade liberalization led to lower inflation and a smaller trade deficit and at the same time increased the levels of private investment and total output. Based on these empirical findings Conway concludes that "If only one form of trade liberalization is possible, a country with Turkey's characteristics and import-substitution heritage may well find that imported-input liberalization should have priority" (p. 62).

This assessment does not differ intransigently from other policy conclusions on this subject. It is generally agreed that devaluation could contract the economy through supply-side responses and that such contractions may disappear in the long run or be moderated by countercyclical discretionary and income policies (van Wijnbergen 1986; Solimano 1986). An important question to determine, however, is if the economy can respond favorably to passive exchange rate management. For example, governments may intentionally attempt to reduce inflation by slowing down exchange rate depreciation; at the same time they may attempt to delay the absorption adjustment. Will this be a desirable strategy? In a recent study, Helpman and Razin (1987) deal with this issue and show how such policy-induced delays are likely to create more overvalued currency, more spending, and a larger trade deficit which, in turn, may call for larger devaluations and contractionary responses in future periods. The outcome would be less damaging, however, were the necessary absorption policies implemented in a timely manner.

Thus it is possible that exchange rate policies, whether they are delayed or frequently used, may negate the residual outcome of trade liberalization policies. To moderate the negative outcomes in either case it may be necessary to design a realistic exchange rate strategy in coordination with an appropriate absorption policy.

Kumcu introduces such a policy alternative. When countries face payment crises and at the same time intentionally delay their exchange rate and absorption policy adjustments, other things being equal, domestic prices will increase, income will shrink, and so will the trade deficit. This leads to the view that the Turkish government can, indeed, influence the investment level, output growth, and inflation rate. Turkish lira may be allowed to depreciate and the interest rate to rise, both leading to higher output and lower inflation.[1]

Before proceeding with this review it is necessary to point out the seemingly contradictory results of the preceding discussion. While Conway argues against devaluation as a possible trade liberalization strategy, Kumcu makes a strong case for it, especially when devaluation is accommodated by a real interest-rate policy. More interesting, Conway shows declining levels of output and investment caused mainly by frequent devaluations, while Kumcu demonstrates higher output and lower inflation.

The differences are explicit at the methodological level.[2] Using a fairly comprehensive model, Conway captures the output and price effects of devaluation in isolation. Kumcu, on the other hand, derives conclusions from a four-equation, four-variable model, interpreting the devaluation reality from the combined influences of specified and omitted variables. However, both models are exact in terms of what they intend to accomplish. While one captures the impact of devaluation in isolation, the other establishes a useful policy link between the real interest rate and the real exchange rate with a relatively less detailed specification of the determinants of output growth and inflation.

Liberalization, Growth, and Inflation

In Chapter 5, Fry examines the negative relationship between Turkey's inflation and growth over the period 1951-85. The inflation of this period seems to be associated with large foreign exchange receipts. Central Bank expands domestic credit and accelerates monetary growth in response to the inflow of foreign exchange. This sets the stage for the inflationary cycle; inflationary expectations begin to form and budget deficits grow due to delays in revenue collection and erosion of the tax base in the public sector. When the deficit is set to be monetized, domestic credit and monetary growth accelerate, escalating the rate of inflation.

The dynamics of this process lead to reduced growth. The ratio of the actual to expected price levels first increases due to a larger money supply, then declines in response to increased expectations of inflation. In addition, the deposit rate, demand for money, and credit supply all begin to decline in real terms, resulting in a severe credit squeeze. It was this shortage of credit that was responsible for Turkey's reduced capital utilization and lower rates of growth.

Fry captures these dynamics quite well with a dynamic simulation of Turkey's money supply process. One major conclusion from his study is that the real deposit rate could be used fairly effectively as a policy instrument to reduce inflation and stimulate growth. The increase in the real deposit rate of interest raises money demand; this alone reduces inflation and relieves the credit squeeze, positively affecting economic growth. Fry argues that ". . . the substantial increases in deposit rates were mainly responsible for Turkey's relatively small recession and reasonably rapid recovery after the stabilization program was initiated in 1980" (p. 107).

Note that further raises in the real deposit rate could be the cause of higher inflation while simultaneously stimulating growth. Before 1983 the association between inflation and the real deposit rate was negative. However, as Fry notes in his concluding remarks, "When adjustments started to be made more frequently after 1983, the negative association disappeared, as did the negative association between inflation or monetary growth and the rate of economic growth" (p. 109).

Fry's conclusions do not fundamentally differ from those reached by others. Gazioglu (1986), Öniş (1986), Aktan and Baysan (1985), and Ertuna (1986) share similar views concerning the dynamics of inflation in Turkey. In addition to such internal inflation causing factors as monetization of budget deficits, lags in price setting, and delays in tax collection (Gazioglu 1986), the growing gap between domestic saving and investment

(Ertuna 1986), and corrective inflation induced by the liberalization of key relative prices (Öniş 1986), they also point out external factors, in particular the oil crisis and the other supply shocks caused by the worldwide stagflation of the 1980s. Among the several policy instruments that can be used to combat inflation, these authors suggest controlling the volume of credit and other fiscal measures to restrain public investments (Ertuna 1986), increasing efficiency and productivity in the public sector (Gazioglu 1986), and raising the allocative efficiency and improving the operation of the free market (Aktan and Baysan 1985).

Another suggestion, which would raise allocational efficiency and moderate the adverse impact of real interest-rate variations, is to carry out the necessary financial reforms. Analyzing Turkey's post-1982 experience with rising interest rates and citing the bankruptcy of the major brokerage houses, Rittenberg signifies the necessity of financial liberalization. Inselbag and Gültekin, with their detailed account of Turkey's financial system, confirm Rittenberg's recommendation. According to these authors, Turkey's financial markets lack basic institutions and instruments and are in dire need of fundamental restructuring if they are to perform at the same level of operational and allocational efficiency as their counterparts do in developed markets.

Inselbag and Gültekin propose several policy measures: (1) the liberalization of interest rates to achieve rational and equitable allocating of loanable funds; (2) introduction of new financial configurations in the primary and secondary markets; (3) development of financial information sharing and standardized accounting systems; and (4) promotion and development of equity markets. These measures would create an environment that would widen and deepen the financial markets and invite direct foreign investment and foreign funds.

Direct Foreign Investment and the Debt Burden

One of the pressing goals of the liberalization package was to attract direct foreign investment (DFI) to moderate financial pressures resulting from the savings gap in Turkey. Much has been done in this area. Despite recent increases in the volume of DFI, however, overall performance to date is hardly satisfactory. As

Erdilek writes in Chapter 8, Turkey's political and economic environments continue to present shortcomings detrimental to attracting foreign capital. Therefore, to compete for the attention of risk conscious foreign investors, Turkey must continue to gain credibility.[3] Most important, continuity and consistency in the implementation of liberalization measures must be maintained, since, as Erdilek concludes, "(The) durability of (liberalization) is in doubt due to both the government's own unstable policymaking and the uneven pace of the economy's development. These two factors are, of course, interrelated with political instability, which also weighs heavily in the minds of foreign investors" (p. 156).

Similar concerns are raised in Chapter 9. As highlighted by Rodrik, standby agreements from the IMF and special assistance under OECD auspices were the main contributing factors that eased Turkey's debt burden. Supplemented by domestic price and fiscal stabilization programs, Turkey improved its current account position and by the mid-1980s managed to become a lower risk country, an eligible voluntary borrower, and a creditworthy participant in international financial markets.

The majority of other debtor countries, in particular Latin American countries, were unable to enjoy similar support (Sachs 1986). Consequently, their delayed adjustment to the crisis was much more worrisome. Unfavorable domestic factors, such as severe public-sector deficits, easy monetary and credit policies, and a decline in domestic capital formation, were exacerbated by the global recession of 1981-82, an overvalued dollar, high interest rates, and other external factors that delay a satisfactory solution to the problem (Cline 1985; Wiesner 1985).

As of today, despite unfavorable domestic investment and growth levels and economic uncertainties, the global debt problem seems to have stabilized, but the problem of solvency remains.[4] Unless acceptable debt management compatible with long-term economic growth is sustained, the deterioration in both external and internal factors could easily provoke another international financial crisis (Orlando and Teitel 1986).

It is noteworthy that within such an international financial environment Turkey has managed to normalize its creditworthiness and continue orderly repayments. For Turkey to continue to serve its debts or remain a legitimate voluntary borrower, continuity in domestic stabilization and liberalization programs must be maintained. In particular, fiscal stability and export diversification must be achieved. Despite any short-term deterioration in internal or external economic conditions, continuing efforts should be made to maintain reforms and pursue outward-looking policies on efficient grounds. As Wiesner notes, "The issue . . . is how to preserve long-term efficiency when short-term and urgent pressures make it attractive to reduce openness and to seek economic reactivation through protectionism" (1985:195).

It is also important that we seriously consider Rodrik's warnings concerning the debt management practices that have recently been retiring long-term debt by converting it to short-term. This practice not only increases servicing costs through higher interest rates, but it also raises the volume of outstanding debt, subjecting Turkey to an overhang of the debt problem. It has been shown that because of a substantial debt overhang, debtor countries will not only face difficulties in raising funds from external and internal markets but will also be unable to avoid capital flight (Sachs 1986; Wiesner 1985). In either case, domestic investments are likely to collapse and thus stagnate the export earnings and growth that are so vital for continuing recovery and development.

While at this time such developments may seem a remote possibility in Turkey, one should not overlook the potential of adverse effects on investment, growth, and exports. Moreover, a supply shock of a 1974-75 intensity and a slowdown in OECD growth could very well renew the debt crisis, enlarge the budget deficit, raise inflation, deteriorate the exchange rate, and revive the political instability of the 1970s.

It is clear that at this juncture, Turkey must strive to sustain a steadily growing economy, generate new capacity, and gradually reduce the debt-service burden. However, in view of shrinking external markets and increased protectionism in industrial nations, these do not seem easy goals to achieve. As Rodrik concludes, "The challenge for the future will be to maintain the recovery without damaging overall confidence in the state of the economy. Any semblance of a confidence crisis could set the economy back several years by bringing private capital inflows to a virtual standstill" (p. 181).

We conclude this section with the following observations:

1. Frequent devaluations are counterproductive. While helping the trade balance, they tend to slow down the economy by lowering investments, simultaneously generating high rates of inflation and unemployment. The other extreme--passive exchange rate management--is also counterproductive. By slowing down exchange rate adjustment, the authorities may create overvalued currency and generate excessive spending, leading to larger trade deficits, which again may require future devaluations.
2. A realistic exchange rate strategy in coordination with an appropriate macropolicy could moderate the negative outcomes of trade liberalization policies. A well-coordinated exchange rate and interest-rate policy, for example, could easily remove the credit squeeze and consequently lower the rate of inflation. Sometimes excessive increases in the interest rate may give rise to high rates of inflation. When that happens, lowering the rate of inflation becomes possible only at the expense of a reduced growth rate.
3. An alternative to ease the credit squeeze and break the resource constraint in Turkey is to explore the possibility of raising an adequate amount of funds from the international capital markets. Although recently Turkey managed to become an eligible voluntary borrower and a creditworthy participant in the international financial markets, this alternative is still problematic. Unfavorable conditions impeding an easy flow of international funds still remain. In particular, the risk of another worldwide stagflation and the problem of stagnating export earnings may again revive the debt crisis and political instability of the 1970s.
4. Political instability and the risk of a renewed confidence crisis also pose a setback for another source of international capital: direct foreign investment, DFI. Despite recent increases in the volume of DFI, Turkey still lacks the confidence of foreign investors. This stems from the uneven pace of the economy's development and uncertainties surrounding the future of liberalization in Turkey.

The inadequacy of social overhead capital is another disadvantage keeping foreign capital at its current levels.

FURTHER EXTENSIONS OF THE LIBERALIZATION PROCESS

The preceding discussion reveals several critical issues that Turkey's economic liberalization needs to resolve. In particular, the problems of unemployment, inflation, and trade and budget deficits require immediate attention. So far, the liberalization strategy has been unsuccessful in controlling the rate of inflation, and despite increased levels of public investment and growth, unemployment remains at one of the highest levels among the OECD nations. Like the budget deficit, the trade balance is negative, with no sign of improvement in the near future.

This situation could improve considerably with the development of new solutions under two distinct policy alternatives. The first alternative suggests an outward-looking strategy under the guidance of a macro plan that would assume the role of setting national targets and priorities.[5] The second alternative involves structural alterations to move the economy beyond the status quo, with measures furthering liberalization and establishing a genuinely competitive free-market economy.

While the specifics of the first strategy are yet to evolve, the idea of intensive planning revives concerns from past implementations and raises doubts about its consistency with an outward-looking development strategy.[6]

The second alternative requires fundamental alterations to improve Turkey's legal, political, and organizational effectiveness. The purpose is to create an environment in which the market functions properly, and individuals enjoy the opportunity of performing freely and productively.[7] More important, such alterations could improve the market orientation of the economy so that both stabilization and liberalization policies can be effectively pursued.[8]

When Turkey's liberalization movement is viewed from the perspective of the second alternative, the outward-looking strategy and all other measures that come with it appear to be consistent. They are necessary but not sufficient to exert enough pressure on the supply side of the economy. Further liberalization will certainly initiate additional gains. More distance could be gained if more emphasis is placed on those measures that may enrich the democratic infrastructure, strengthen the competitive forces of the economy, and raise resource efficiency through the intensive use of society's factors of production.[9]

SUMMARY AND CONCLUDING REMARKS

Turkey's latest liberalization attempt is unique in many respects. Rather than evolving as a gradual progression of the Turkish economic system, it was introduced abruptly and applied as part of an orthodox stabilization package. The package seemed sufficiently extensive and principally gave high priority to trade liberalization. Privatization, interest-rate liberalization, and renovation of the financial markets were further measures advanced for the liberalization of the domestic economy.

The program was initiated to relieve the economy from one of the worst crises in Turkish economic history. Therefore expectations were high. In addition to solving the balance of payments crisis, the liberalization strategy had to resolve the problems of inflation and unemployment and accomplish a transformation from a highly protective and traditionally statist economy to an adequately privatized, export-oriented economy.

So far the experience has been fairly successful. In spite of rising protectionist trends among advanced nations, Turkey firmly reduced trade barriers and almost quadrupled trade volume since 1980. Exports rose considerably, both in quality and quantity. In addition, Turkey managed to normalize its debt situation and, despite high risks and a confidence crisis in international financial markets, become a moderately low risk voluntary borrower.

Regarding the unemployment and inflation rates, however, the situation is not very encouraging. Despite high rates of growth and investment, unemployment is still high; and even though it declined from three-digit levels, inflation seems to have stabilized within the 40 to 60 percentage range. On another front, the trade deficit continues to grow, with occasional warnings urging the renewal of some of the trade barriers.

A strict application of the stabilization measures accompanying the liberalization policies could perhaps better the situation. Calls for more domestic savings and the enactment of carefully coordinated monetary and fiscal policies (well-managed interest rate and exchange rate policies, for example) could improve the performance of the economy. However, the Turkish economy still lacks well-balanced policy and economic environments. Financial institutions and capital markets have yet to mature. The fiscal process is tedious and the budget deficit is unnecessarily large, leaving little room for policymakers to exercise necessary discretionary macro-policies.

Thus, an urgent task for the government is to carry out scheduled reforms. Capital and money markets must be developed along the lines of international standards, and their endurance must be assured against all possible short-term political and economic fluctuations. Likewise, the budget deficit must be reduced to a manageable margin, and more important, the tax code must be strictly enforced. This will not only prevent tax evasion but will also raise the effectiveness of fiscal measures in a free-market economic setting.

Of course, liberalization alone should not be viewed as a panacea for Turkey's immediate macroeconomic problems. Economic liberalism is a system with its own unique problems and a strategy with long-term outcomes. Raising contrary expectations and hastily turning to alternative strategies when expectations remain unfulfilled would be likely to aggrevate already existing problems.

As economic liberalism evolves as a system, it requires a gradual moderation of the role of the state in economic affairs. In an ideal free-market economy, the allocational role of the government is limited to the provision of collective goods. Income redistribution and the establishment of rules and regulations to achieve the highest possible social welfare are also within the range of government's responsibilities. With these primary allocational and distributional functions, governments must, therefore, define and redefine property rights and strive to improve efficiency to achieve the highest possible economic welfare.

It should be noted that reorienting individual expectations along the lines of a contemporary free-market model and accordingly developing state-individual relations is a demanding process. However, the government can play an effective leadership role in this process. Employing the contemporary products of high technology and performing the traditional allocation, distribution, and stabilization functions effectively will earn the government credibility and much needed confidence in the system.

I should note in closing that the present administration in Turkey seems determined to assume such a leadership role, and it has traveled a considerable distance in this respect. One important question, however, remains and needs to be raised while further liberalization measures are still underway.

Is liberalization an appropriate strategy for Turkey at this stage of its economic development? To arrive at a mature answer, one certainly needs to consider all relevant facts and expectations regarding the future of the nation. As we leave behind the worldwide stagflation of the early 1980s, more nations, including those with a collectivist tradition, have been turning to free-market solutions and developing new strategies to ease the orientation of their economies to rapid advances in technology. Turkey, a member of Western democracies and a possible participant in the European Economic Community, has also explored alternative routes and decisively initiated an unprecedented strategy toward a free-market economy. Today, a viable alternative for Turkey is a more structured and improved form of liberalization--a real market economy, with a democratic government interacting with individuals in a contemporary fashion. This does not imply that the market system is free of problems. As any economic system does, it has its own costs and benefits, or as Hirschman writes, ". . . the moral basis of capitalist society will be seen as being constantly depleted and replenished at the same time. An excess of depletion over replenishment and a consequent crisis of the system is then of course possible, but the special circumstances making for it would have to be noted, just as it might be possible to specify conditions under which the system would gain in cohesion and legitimacy" (1983:1483).

NOTES

1. Kumcu's model seems to be driven by the critical assumption of a fixed nominal wage. Under this constraint, domestic prices must fall in order for

output to increase in response to currency depreciation. Falling domestic prices will raise real wages, and this will induce producers to switch to imported intermediate goods to raise output. For the domestic price effects of exchange rate adjustments see Cooper (1971) and Dornbusch (1987).

2. The controversy is less significant at the policy implication level. Both authors agree that devaluation must be accompanied by appropriate domestic policies. This is stated in Kumcu's study and Conway leads the argument in that direction.

3. Some tax incentives, as an optimal means to convey information about productivity levels, could be designed to attract FDI in high productivity sectors (Bond and Samuelson 1986). In addition, more effort could be shown to augment social overhead capital (Rauch 1986). Once FDI starts to be drawn to a country it becomes important that any low-cost advantage is maintained. This can be accomplished by increasing productivity or devaluing the overall foreign exchange rate and reducing the foreign exchange risk (Calderonn-Rossell 1985).

4. In a recent assessment of the situation, Krueger (1987) lists five factors constituting a vicious circle: a rising debt service ratio, low growth rates in debtor countries, low export performances, the failure of policy reforms to go far enough, and rising difficulty in attracting voluntary capital inflows.

5. See Boratav, Keyder, Pamuk (1984); Kafaoglu (1984); Kazgan (1985); and Ulagay (1987).

6. First, maintaining autonomy for those who will be responsible for the coordination of the plan may turn out to be impractical. As has been experienced in the past, planners may end up finding themselves constrained by counterproductive influences and led by the expectations and priorities of political institutions. Second, the economy could gradually switch to inward-looking industrialization, possibly with excessive incentives granted to import substitution industries. Note that returning to such a policy would be inefficient and costly. While the rest of the industrialized world is rapidly moving into a high-tech era, deepening the import substitution industries in Turkey would require substantial physical capital and human resources. It would also deprive the country of the net returns that are yet to be gained from the

current policies of export-oriented, outward-looking industrialization.

7. Gains from this alternative can be attained by restructuring and clarifying the role of the state and redefining its relationship to individuals in compliance with the rules of a competitive market economy. In Turkey, in contrast to free-market economies, individuals form expectations from the perception that the state is in the center of economic life. In addition to providing public goods, governments are viewed as responsible for the production of essential private goods and achieving an acceptable level of social welfare. It is true that the role of the state in Turkey has been changing gradually since the inception of the 1980 liberalization policy. But despite impressive accomplishments, the expectation that the "state does or must do everything" has yet to change.

8. Such efforts will not only help individuals reveal their actual inclinations regarding the use of public resources but will also generate and reinforce market dynamics, which could gradually shift the aggregate supply curve to much desired levels.

9. Redefining and defining property rights and increasing their congruence with the norms and the dynamics of the free-market system is another area in which substantial improvement in economic efficiency may be attained. As market dynamics begin to dominate economic life and assume the role of allocating society's resources, the interrelationship among economic agents becomes increasingly complex, requiring new rules and regulations for the internalization of likely externalities. For example, as discussed in Benjamin and Duvall, the rights in developing countries are basic, ". . . centered on the 'life, liberty, and property' trinity, with particular emphasis on the material dimensions. In the extreme, they reduce almost entirely to property rights" (1985:37). In an advanced industrial society, however, rights are much more differentiated and interdependent, and they relate mostly to quality-of-life issues. It is within this latter context that Turkey may begin to view individual liberties and assess the relevance of existing and potential collective controls.

REFERENCES

Aktan, O., and T. Baysan. 1985. Integration of the Turkish economy into the world economy: Trade liberalization, comparative advantage and optimum policies. *METU Studies in Development* 12(1-2): 49-106.

Benjamin, R., and R. Duvall. 1985. The capitalist state in context. In *The Democratic State*, edited by R. Benjamin and S. L. Elkin, 19-58. Lawrence: University of Kansas Press.

Bond, E. W., and L. Samuelson. 1986. Tax holidays as signals. *American Economic Review* 76:820-26.

Boratav, K., C. Keyder, and S. Pamuk. 1984. *Krizin Gelisimi Ve Turkiye'nin Alternatif Sorunu.* Istanbul: Kaynak Yayinlari.

Calderonn-Rossell, J. R. 1985. Towards the theory of foreign direct investment. *Oxford Economic Papers* 37:282-91.

Cline, W. R. 1985. International debt: From crisis to recovery. *American Economic Review Proceedings* 75:185-90.

Cooper, R. 1971. Currency devaluation in developing countries. *Princeton Essays in International Finance* 86:3-31.

Dornbusch, R. 1987. Exchange rate management. *American Economic Review* 77:93-106.

Ertuna, O. 1986. The macroeconomic stability: The Turkish case 1950-1979. *Yapi Kredi Economic Review* 1(1):93-108.

Gazioglu, S. 1986. Government deficits, consumption and inflation in Turkey. *METU Studies in Development* 13(1-2):117-34.

Helpman, E., and A. Razin. 1987. Exchange rate management. *American Economic Review* 77:107-23.

Hirschman, A. O. 1982. Rival interpretations of market society: Civilizing, destructive, or feeble? *Journal of Economic Literature* 20:1463-84.

Kafaoglu, A. B. 1984. *Iste Alternatif: Demokratik Planli Kalkinma.* Istanbul: Alan Yayincilik.

Kazgan, G. 1985. *Ekonomide Disa Acik Buyume.* Istanbul: Altin Kitaplar.

Krueger, A. O. 1987. Debt, capital flows, and LDC growth. *American Economic Review Proceedings* 77:159-64.

Öniş, Z. 1986. Stabilization and growth in a semi-industrial economy: An evaluation of the recent Turkish experiment, 1977-1984. *METU Studies in Development* 13(1-2):7-28.

Orlando, F., and S. Teitel. 1986. Latin America's external debt problem: Debt servicing strategies compatible with long-term economic growth. *Economic Development and Cultural Change* 34:641-71.

Rauch, J. E. 1986. The transfer of production from rich to poor countries. *Journal of Development Economics* 23:41-53.

Sachs, J. 1986. Managing the LDC debt crisis. *Brookings Papers on Economic Activity* 2:397:431.

Solimano, A. 1986. Devaluation in the Southern Cone: The case of Chili. *Journal of Development Economics* 23:131-51.

Ulagay, O. 1987. *Kim Kazandi Kim Kaybetti.* Ankara: Bilgi Yayinevi.

van Wijnbergen, S. 1986. Exchange rate and stabilization policies in LDCs. *Journal of Development Economics* 23:227-47.

Wiesner, E. 1985. Latin American debt: Lessons and pending issues. *American Economic Review Proceedings* 75:191-95.

Bibliography

Abe, S., M. J. Fry, B. K. Min, P. Vongvipanond, and T.-P. Yu. 1975. The demand for money in Pakistan: Some alternative estimates. *Pakistan Development Review* 14(2):249-57.

Aghevli, B., and M. Khan. 1977. Inflationary finance and the dynamics of inflation: Indonesia, 1951-72. *American Economic Review* 67(3):390-403.

______. 1978. Government deficits and the inflationary process in developing countries. *International Monetary Fund Staff Papers* 25(3):383-416.

Aktan, O., and T. Baysan. 1985. Integration of the Turkish economy into the world economy: Trade liberalization, comparative advantage and optimum policies. *METU Studies in Development* 12(1-2): 49-106.

Alexander, S. 1952. Effects of a devaluation on a trade balance. *IMF Staff Papers* 2:263-78.

Balassa, B. 1982. *Development Strategies in Semi-Industrial Economies*. Baltimore: Johns Hopkins Press.

______. 1984. Adjustment policies in developing countries: A reassessment. *World Development*. 12(9):955-72.

Benjamin, R., and R. Duvall. 1985. The capitalist state in context. In *The Democratic State*, edited by R. Benjamin and S. L. Elkin, 19-58. Lawrence: University of Kansas Press.

Berksoy, T. 1982. Turkiye'de istikrar arayislari ve IMF. In *IMF Istikrar Politikalari ve Turkiye*, edited by C. Erdost. Ankara: Savaş Yayinlari.

Bhagwati, J., and H. G. Johnson. 1961. The generalized theory of the effects of tariffs on the terms of trade. *Oxford Economic Papers* 13:225-53.

Black, S. W. 1983. The use of monetary policy for internal and external balance in ten industrial countries. In *Exchange Rates and International Macroeconomics*, edited by J. A. Frenkel, 189-225. Chicago: University of Chicago Press.

Bond, E. W., and L. Samuelson. 1986. Tax holidays as signals. *American Economic Review* 76:820-26.

Boratav, K., C. Keyder, and S. Pamuk. 1984. *Krizin Gelisimi Ve Turkiye'nin Alternatif Sorunu.* Istanbul: Kaynak Yayinlari.

Brecher, R. A. 1974. Minimum wage rates and the pure theory of international trade. *Quarterly Journal of Economics* 88:98-116.

Brito, D. L., and J. D. Richardson. 1975. Some disequilibrium dynamics of exchange rate changes. *Journal of International Economics* 5:1-13.

Bruno, M., and J. Sachs. 1979. Macro-economic adjustment with import price shocks: Real and monetary aspects. National Bureau of Economic Research Working Paper 340. Cambridge, Mass.: NBER.

______. 1985. *Economics Of Worldwide Stagflation.* Cambridge: Harvard University Press.

Buffie, E. F. 1984a. Financial repression, the new structuralists, and stabilization policy in semi-industrial economies. *Journal of Development Economics* 14(3):305-22.

______. 1984b. Macroeconomics of trade liberalization. *Journal of International Economics* 17:121-37.

Calderonn-Rossell, J. R. 1985. Towards the theory of foreign direct investment. *Oxford Economic Papers* 37:282-91.

Calvo, G. A. 1986. Fractured liberalism: Argentina under Martinez de Hoz. *Economic Development and Cultural Change* 3:511-33.

______. 1987. On the costs of temporary liberalization/stabilization experiments. In *Economic Reform and Liberalization in Latin America*, edited by M. Connolly and C. Gonzales-Vega, 3-17. New York: Praeger.

Canevi, Y. 1984. Role of stabilization policies in the world debt problem: The Turkish experience. Speech delivered at the conference on LDC Financing--Managing the Way Back, 6-9 May, at the Federal Reserve Bank of New York, New York City.

Celasun, M. 1986. Income distribution and domestic terms of trade in Turkey, 1978-1983. *METU Studies in Development* 13(1-2):193-216.

Central Bank of the Republic of Turkey. *Annual Report*. Various issues. Ankara.

______. 1984. *Uc Aylik Istatistik Ozetleri*. Ankara, March.

______. 1984. *Information Memorandum*. Ankara, June.

______. 1986. *Monthly Statistical and Evaluation Bulletin*. Ankara, June.

Chacholiades, M. 1978. *International Trade Theory and Policy*. New York: McGraw-Hill.

Choksi, A. 1986. Adjustment with growth in the highly indebted middle-income countries. CPD discussion paper 1986-36. Washington, D.C.: The World Bank.

Cline, W. R. 1982. Can the East Asian model of

development be generalized? *World Development* 11:81-90.

______. 1985. International debt: From crisis to recovery. *American Economic Review Proceedings* 75:185-90.

Cline, W. R., and S. Weintraub, eds. 1981. *Economic Stabilization in Developing Countries*. Washington, D.C.: The Brookings Institution.

Çölaşan, E. 1983. *24 Ocak, Bir Donemin Perde Arkasi*. Istanbul: Milliyet Yayinlari.

Conway, P. 1986. Decomposing the determinants of trade deficits: Turkey in the 1970s. *Journal of Development Economics* 22:235-58.

______. 1987. *Economic Shocks and Structural Adjustments: Turkey after* 1973. Amsterdam: North Holland.

Cooper, R. 1971. Currency devaluation in developing countries. *Princeton Essays in International Finance* 86:3-31.

Corbo, V., J. de Melo, and J. Tybout. 1986. What went wrong with recent reforms in the Southern Cone? *Economic Development and Cultural Change* 3:606-40.

Corbo, V., and F. Ossa. 1985. Small open economies: The main issues. In *Export-Oriented Development Strategies: The Success of Five Newly Industrializing Countries*, edited by V. Corbo, A. Krueger and F. Ossa, 5-16. Boulder, Colo.: Westview Press.

Çoşan, F. M., and H. Ersel. 1987. Turkish financial system: Its evolution and performance 1980-86. Research and Development Department, Capital Market Board. Ankara.

Dell, S. 1984. A note on stabilization and the World Bank. *World Development* 12:165-67.

de Melo, J., and J. Tybout. 1986. The effects of financial liberalization on savings and investment in

Uruguay. *Economic Development and Cultural Change* 34(3):561-87.

Derviş, K., and P. Petri. 1987. The macroeconomics of successful development: What are the lessons? Paper presented for the NBER Conference on Macroeconomics, March 13-14, Cambridge, Mass.

Diaz-Alejandro, C. 1985. Good-bye financial repression, hello financial crash. *Journal of Development Economics* 19:1-24.

Dornbusch, R. 1980. *Open-Economy Macroeconomics.* New York: Basic Books.

______. 1984. Argentina since Martinez de Hoz. National Bureau of Economic Research Working Paper 1466. Cambridge, Mass.: NBER.

______. 1987. Exchange rate management. *American Economic Review* 77:93-106.

DPT (State Planning Organization). 1986. *1986 Yili Programi* (1986 Annual Program). Ankara.

Dutton, D. S. 1971. A model of self-generating inflation: The Argentine case. *Journal of Money, Credit and Banking* 3(2):245-62.

Edwards, S. 1985. Stabilization with liberalization: An evaluation of ten years of Chile's experiment with free-market policies, 1973-83. *Economic Development and Cultural Change* 33:223-54.

Edwards, S., and S. van Wijnbergen. 1986. The order of liberalization of the current and capital accounts of the balance of payments. In *Economic Liberalization in Developing Countries*, edited by A. Choksi and D. Papageorgiou, 185-223. New York: Basil Blackwell.

______. 1987. On the appropriate timing and speed of economic liberalization in developing countries. In *Economic Reform and Liberalization in Latin America*, edited by M. Connolly and C. Gonzalez-Vega, 71-92. New York: Praeger.

Ekzen, N. 1984. 1980 stabilizasyon paketinin 1958, 1970 ve 1978-1979 paketleri ile karsilastirmali analizi. In *Turkiye'de ve Dunyada Yasanan Ekonomik Bunalim*, edited by I. Tekeli, et al. Ankara: Yurt Yayinlari.

Erdilek, A.. 1982. *Direct Foreign Investment in Turkish Manufacturing: An Analysis of the Conflicting Objectives and Frustrated Expectations of a Host Country*. Tübingen: J.C.B. Mohr.

______. 1985. The dynamics of the foreign direct investment environment in Turkey. In *Political Risks in International Business: New Directions for Research, Management and Public Policy*, edited by T. L. Brewer. New York: Praeger.

______. 1986. Turkey's new open-door policy of direct foreign investment: A critical analysis of problems and prospects. *METU Studies in Development* 13(1-2): 171-91.

Ertuna, O. 1986. The macroeconomic stability: The Turkish case 1950-1979. *Yapi Kredi Economic Review* 1(1):93-108.

Euromoney, February 1986.

Feder, G. 1982. On exports and economic growth. *World Bank Staff Paper 508*. Washington, D.C.: The World Bank.

Findlay, R., and C. Rodriguez. 1977. Intermediate imports and macroeconomic policy under flexible exchange rates. *Canadian Journal of Economics* 10:208-17.

Fleming, M. 1962. Domestic financial policies under fixed and floating exchange rates. *International Monetary Fund Staff Paper* 9:369-79.

Fry, M. J. 1971. Turkey's first five-year development plan: An assessment. *Economic Journal* 81(322): 306-26.

______. 1972. *Finance and Development Planning in*

Turkey. Leiden: Brill.

______. 1978a. Alternative stabilization strategies from a model of short-run price and output fluctuations in Turkey. *METU Studies in Development* 5(18):21-36.

______. 1978b. Further investigation into Turkey's Phillips curve. *METU Studies in Development* 5(19):66-88.

______. 1978c. Money and capital or financial deepening in economic development? *Journal of Money, Credit and Banking* 10(4):464-75.

______. 1979. The cost of financial repression in Turkey. *Saving and Development* 3(2):127-35.

______. 1980a. Saving, investment, growth and the cost of financial repression. *World Development* 8(4):317-27.

______. 1980b. Money, interest, inflation and growth in Turkey. *Journal of Monetary Economics* 6(4):535-45.

______. 1981. Inflation and economic growth in Pacific basin developing economies. *Federal Reserve Bank of San Francisco Economic Review* (Fall):8-18.

______. 1982a. Models of financially repressed developing economies. *World Development* 10(9):731-50.

______. 1982b. Analysing disequilibrium interest-rate systems in developing countries. *World Development* 10(12):1049-57.

______. 1984. Saving, financial intermediation and economic growth in Asia. *Asian Development Review* 2(1):82-91.

______. 1986a. Terms-of-trade dynamics in Asia: An analysis of national saving and domestic investment responses to terms-of-trade changes in 14 Asian LDCs. *Journal of International Money and Finance* 5(1):57-73.

______. 1986b. Turkey's great inflation. *METU Studies in*

Development 13(1-2):95-116.

Fry, M. J., and M. R. Farhi. 1979. *Money and Banking in Turkey.* Istanbul: Bogazici University Press.

Gazioglu, S. 1986. Government deficits, consumption and inflation in Turkey. *METU Studies in Development* 13(1-2):117-34.

Giersch, H. 1986. *The International Debt Problem: Lessons for the Future.* Tübingen: J.C.B. Mohr.

Giovannini, A. 1983. The interest elasticity of savings in developing countries: The existing evidence. *World Development* 11(7):601-7.

Gültekin, B., and I. Inselbag. 1985. Financial markets in Turkey. Paper presented at the eleventh annual meeting of the Eastern Economic Association. Pittsburgh, March 21-23.

Helpman, E., and A. Razin. 1987. Exchange rate management. *American Economic Review* 77:107-23.

Hemphill, W. L. 1974. The effect of foreign exchange receipts on imports of less developed countries. *International Monetary Fund Staff Papers* 21(3):637-77.

Hirschman, A. O. 1982. Rival interpretations of market society: Civilizing, destructive, or feeble? *Journal of Economic Literature* 20:1463-84.

International Currency Analysis Inc. 1986. *World Currency Yearbook.* Washington, D.C.

International Finance Corporation. 1986. *Annual Report 1986.* Washington, D.C.

International Labor Organization. *Labor Statistics Yearbook.* Various issues. Washington, D.C.

International Monetary Fund. 1977. *The Monetary Approach to the Balance of Payments.* Washington, D.C.: International Monetary Fund.

______. 1981. *Annual Report on Exchange Arrangements and Exchange Restrictions,* 1981. Washington, D.C.: International Monetary Fund.

______. 1982a. *Exchange Arrangements and Exchange Restrictions, Annual Report 1982.* Washington, D.C.: International Monetary Fund.

______. 1982b. Turkey--review of stand-by arrangement and exchange system. EBS/82/130. Washington, D.C.: International Monetary Fund.

______. 1984. *Balance of Payments Manual.* 4th ed., Washington, D.C.: International Monetary Fund.

______. 1985a. *Exchange Arrangements and Exchange Restrictions, Annual Report 1985.* Washington, D.C.: International Monetary Fund.

______. 1985b. *Foreign Private Investment in Developing Countries*, Washington, D.C.: International Monetary Fund.

______. 1986a. *International Capital Markets.* Washington, D.C.: International Monetary Fund.

______. 1986b. *International Capital Markets.* Washington, D.C.: International Monetary Fund.

______. *International Financial Statistics.* Various Issues. Washington, D.C.: International Monetary Fund.

Johnson, H. G. 1972. The monetary approach to balance-of-payments theory. In *Further Essays in Monetary Economics*, by H. G. Johnson. London: Allen & Unwin.

Kafaoglu, A. B. 1984. *Iste Alternatif: Demokratik Planli Kalkinma.* Istanbul: Alan Yayincilik.

______. 1986. *DCM Dosyasi.* Istanbul.

Kapur, B. K. 1976. Alternative stabilization policies for less-developed economies. *Journal of Political Economy* 84(4):777-95.

Kazgan, G. 1985. *Ekonomide Disa Acik Buyume.* Istanbul: Altin Kitaplar.

Keller, P. M. 1980. Implications of credit policies for output and the Balance of Payments. *International Monetary Fund Staff Papers* 27(3):451-77.

Khan, M., and R. Zahler. 1987. The liberalization of trade and capital flows in developing countries: Some theoretical and empirical issues. In *Economic Reform and Liberalization in Latin America*, edited by M. Connolly and C. Gonzalez-Vega, 45-67. New York: Praeger.

Kopits, G.. 1984. Interest rate liberalization and demand for money in Turkey. International Monetary Fund DM/84/32. Washington, D.C.

______. 1987. Structural reform, stabilization and growth in Turkey. International Monetary Fund Occasional Paper Series 52. Washington, D.C.: IMF.

Korteweg, P. 1978. The economics of inflation and output fluctuations in the Netherlands, 1954-1975: A test of some implications of the dominant impulse-cum-rational Expectations Hypothesis. *Journal of Monetary Economics* (supplement 8):17-79.

Krueger, A. O. 1974. *Foreign Trade Regimes and Economic Development: Turkey.* New York: National Bureau of Economic Research.

______. 1978a. *Foreign Trade Regimes and Economic Development: Liberalization Attempts and Consequences.* New York: Columbia University Press.

______. 1978b. *Liberalization Attempts and Consequences.* New York: NBER.

______. 1985. The experience and lessons of Asia's super exporters. In *Export-Oriented Development Strategies: The Success of Five Newly Industrializing Countries*, edited by V. Corbo, A. Kruger, and F. Ossa, 187-212. Boulder, Colo.: Westview Press.

______. 1987a. Debt, capital flows, and LDC growth. *American Economic Review Proceedings* 77:159-64.

______. 1987b. The importance of economic policy in development: Contrasts between Korea and Turkey. National Bureau of Economic Research Working Paper 2195. Cambridge, Mass.: NBER.

Krugman, P., and L. Taylor. 1978. Contractionary effects of devaluation. *Journal of International Economics* 8:445-56.

Kumcu, M. E. 1985. The theory of commercial policy in a monetary economy with sticky wages. *Journal of International Economics* 18:159-70.

Laidler, D. 1978. Money and money income: An essay on the "transmission mechanism". *Journal of Monetary Economics* 4(2):151-91.

Lasker, D. M. 1983. Short-run independence of monetary policy under a pegged exchange-rate system: An econometric approach. In *The International Transmission of Inflation*, edited by M. R. Darby, J. R. Lothian, et. al., 314-48. Chicago: University of Chicago Press for the National Bureau of Economic Research.

Leff, N. H., and K. Sato. 1980. Macroeconomic adjustment in developing countries: Instability, short-run growth, and external dependency. *Review of Economics and Statistics* 22(2):170-9.

Lucas, R. E., Jr. 1973. Some international evidence on output-inflation tradeoffs. *American Economic Review* 63(3):326-34.

Marion, N., and L. Svensson. 1984. World equilibrium and oil price: An intertemporal analysis. *Oxford Economic Papers* 36(1):86-102.

Mathieson, D. J.. 1979. Financial reform and capital flows in a developing economy. IMF *Staff Papers* 26(3):450-89.

______. 1980. Financial reform and stabilization policy

in a developing economy. *Journal of Development Economics* 7(3):359-95.

McKinnon, R. I. 1973. *Money and Capital in Economic Development*. Washington, D.C.: The Brookings Institution.

Michealy, M. 1986. The timing and sequencing of a trade liberalization policy. In *Economic Liberalization in Developing Countries*, edited by A. Choksi and D. Papageorgiou, 41-59. New York: Basil Blackwell.

Mikesell, R. F., and J. E. Zinser. 1973. The nature of the savings function in developing countries: A survey of the theoretical and empirical literature. *Journal of Economic Literature* 11(1):1-26.

Milanovic, B. 1986. Export incentives and Turkish manufactured exports, 1980-84. World Bank Staff Paper 768. Washington, D.C.: The World Bank.

Ministry of Finance. *Annual Economic Report*. Various issues. Ankara.

Mundell, R. A. 1968. *International Economics*. London: Macmillan.

Ness, W. L. 1972. Some effects of inflation on financing investment in Argentina and Brazil. In *Financial Development and Economic Growth: The Economic Consequences of Underdeveloped Capital Markets*, edited by A. W. Sametz, 228-54. New York: New York University Press.

Öniş, Z. 1986. Stabilization and growth in a semi-industrial economy: An evaluation of the recent Turkish experiment, 1977-1984. *METU Studies in Development* 13(1-2):7-28.

Organization for Economic Cooperation and Development. *Turkey--Annual Economic Survey*. Various issues. Paris: OECD.

______. *National Accounts 1960-85*. Paris: OECD.

Orlando, F., and S. Teitel. 1986. Latin America's

external debt problem: Debt servicing strategies compatible with long-term economic growth. *Economic Development and Cultural Change* 34:641-71.

Özal, T. 1986. *Speech to YASED.* Istanbul: YASED.

Papanek, G. F. 1973. Aid, foreign private investment, savings, and growth in less developed countries. *Journal of Political Economy* 81(1):120-30.

Ramazanoglu, H. 1985. The politics of industrialization in a closed economy and the IMF intervention of 1979. In *Turkey in the World Capitalist System*, edited by H. Ramazanoglu. Aldershot Eng.: Gower.

Rauch, J. E. 1986. The transfer of production from rich to poor countries. *Journal of Development Economics* 23:41-53.

Robinson, J. 1947. *Essays in the Theory of Unemployment.* Oxford: Blackwell.

Rodrik, D. 1986. Macroeconomic policy and debt in Turkey during the 1970s: A tale of two policy phases. John F. Kennedy School of Government Discussion Paper 157D, Harvard University.

Roe, A. R. 1982. High interest rates: A new conventional wisdom for development policy? Some conclusions from Sri Lankan experience. *World Development* 10(3):211-22.

Sachs, J. 1981. The current account and macroeconomic adjustment in the 1970s. *Brookings Papers on Economic Activity.* 1:201-68.

______. 1985. External debt and macroeconomic performance in Latin America and East Asia. *Brookings Papers On Economic Activity* 2:523-64.

______. 1986. Managing the LDC debt crisis. *Brookings Papers on Economic Activity* 2:397-431.

Salter, W. 1959. Internal and external balance: The role of price and expenditure effects. *Economic Record* 35(71):226-38.

Saracoglu, R. 1985. The role of real exchange rates in stabilization policies: The case of Turkey. Paper presented at a colloquium for the executive directors of the World Bank, November, Washington, D.C.

Şenses, F. 1981. Short-term stabilization policies in a developing economy: The Turkish experience in 1980 in long-term perspective. *METU Studies in Development* 8(1-2):409-52.

______. 1983. An assessment of Turkey's liberalization attempts since 1980 against the background of her stabilization program. *METU Studies in Development* 10(3):271-322.

Shaw, E. S. 1973. Financial deepening in economic development. New York: Oxford University Press.

Sims, C. A. 1980a. Macroeconomics and reality. *Econometrica* 48:1-48.

______. 1980b. Comparison of interwar and postwar business cycles: Monetarism reconsidered. *American Economic Review* 70:250-57.

Solimano, A. 1986. Devaluation in the Southern Cone: The case of Chili. *Journal of Development Economics* 23:131-51.

Sönmez, M. 1982. *Turkiye Ekonomisinde Bunalim* 2d. ed. Istanbul: Belge Yayinlari.

State Institute of Statistics. 1983. *Statistical Yearbook of Turkey, 1983*. Ankara.

______. 1984. *Monthly Economic Indicators*. Ankara, February.

Svensson, L., and A. Razin. 1983. The terms of trade and the current account: The Harberger-Laursen-Metzler effect. *Journal of Political Economy* 91(1):97-125.

Swan, T. 1963. Longer-run problems of the balance of payments. In *The Australian Economy*, edited by H. Arndt and W. Corden, 349-95. Melbourne: Cheshire

Press.

Taylor, L. 1983. *Structuralist Macroeconomics: Applicable Models for the Third World.* New York: Basic Books.

Tekbaş, M. 1987. Sermaye piyasasi. *Banka ve Ekonomik Yorumlar.* Istanbul.

T. C. Resmi Gazete (Official Gazette of the Turkish Republic). Various issues. Ankara.

Tigrel, A. 1986. *An Overview of the Turkish Economy.* Istanbul: YASED.

Turkish Industrialists' and Businessmen's Association, TUSIAD. 1986. *Turkish Economy 1986.* Istanbul.

Ulagay, O., 1983. *24 Ocak Deneyimi Uzerine.* Istanbul: Hil Yayin.

______. 1987. *Kim Kazandi Kim Kaybetti.* Ankara: Bilgi Yayinevi.

Uluatam, F. A. 1973. *Monetary Multipliers and a Self Generating Inflation Model: The Turkish Case.* Ankara: Turkish Republic State Planning Organization.

van Wijnbergen, S. 1982. Stagflationary effects of monetary stabilization policies: A quantitative analysis of South Korea. *Journal of Development Economics* 10:133-69.

______. 1983. Credit policy, inflation and growth in a financially repressed economy. *Journal of Development Economics* 13:45-65.

______. 1984. The optimal investment and current account response to oil price shocks under putty-clay technology. *Journal of International Economics* 17:138-47.

______. 1986. Exchange rate management and stabilization policies in developing countries. *Journal of Development Economics* 23:227-47

Watson, M., et al. 1986. *International Capital Markets.* Washington, D.C.: International Monetary Fund.

Wiesner, E. 1985. Latin American debt: Lessons and pending issues. *American Economic Review Proceedings* 75:191-95.

World Bank. *World Debt Tables.* Various issues. Washington, D.C.: World Bank.

______. *World Development Report.* Various issues. Washington, D.C.: World Bank.

______. *Bank Economic and Social Database.* Washington, D.C.: World Bank.

YASED (Association for Foreign Capital Coordination). 1986a. *Foreign Capital Legislation in Turkey.* Istanbul.

______. 1986b. *Turkiye'de Yabancilarin Vergilendirilmesi* (Taxation of Foreigners in Turkey). Istanbul.

______. 1986c. *Contribution of Foreign Investment to Turkish Economy.* Istanbul.

Index

Editors and Contributors

Fikret Şenses, Middle East Technical University, Ankara, Turkey

Mehmet Odekon, Skidmore College, Saratoga Springs, New York

Patrick Conway, University of North Carolina at Chapel Hill

M. Ercan Kumcu, State University of New York at Binghamton

Maxwell J. Fry, University of California, Irvine

Libby Rittenberg, Lafayette College, Easton, Pennsylvania

Işık Inselbag, The Wharton School of the University of Pennsylvania

N. Bülent Gültekin, The Wharton School of the University of Pennsylvania

Asım Erdilek, Case Western Reserve University, Cleveland Ohio

Dani Rodrik, Harvard University, Cambridge, Massachusetts

Tevfik F. Nas, University of Michigan, Flint